Dream First, Details Later

Dream First, Details Later

How to Quit Overthinking & Make It Happen!

ELLEN MARIE BENNETT

with Sarah Tomlinson

PENGUIN ● PORTFOLIO

Portfolio / Penguin
An imprint of Penguin Random House LLC
penguinrandomhouse.com

Most Portfolio books are available at a discount when purchased in quantity for sales promotions or corporate use. Special editions, which include personalized covers, excerpts, and corporate imprints, can be created when purchased in large quantities. For more information, please call (212) 572-2232 or e-mail specialmarkets@penguinrandomhouse.com. Your local bookstore can also assist with discounted bulk purchases using the Penguin Random House corporate Business-to-Business program. For assistance in locating a participating retailer, e-mail B2B@penguinrandomhouse.com.

Grateful acknowledgment is made for permission to reprint the following:
Pg. 2 photograph by Shayan Asgharnia; pg. 11 photo by Rick Poon; pgs. 72, 77 photos courtesy of Ellen Bennet; pgs. 97, 136 bottom, endpaper photos copyright © Mary Costa Photography; pgs. 118, 136 top, 137 top, 221 photos courtesy of Hedley & Bennett; pg. 119 photo by Bonnie Tsang; pg. 137 bottom photos courtesy of Caesarstone 5143 White Attica; pg. 157 photo by Lily Glass; pg. 160 photo by Aviv Gattenuo; pg. 224 photo by AnnaMaria Zunino Noellert copyright © AnnaMaria Fotograf; pg. 230 photo by Julia Stotz.

Library of Congress Cataloging-in-Publication Data

Names: Bennett, Ellen (Ellen Marie), author.
Title: Dream first, details later: how to quit overthinking and make it happen / Ellen Bennett.
Description: [New York] : Penguin / Portfolio, [2021]
Identifiers: LCCN 2020034366 (print) | LCCN 2020034367 (ebook) | ISBN 9780593083451 (hardcover) | ISBN 9780593083475 (trade paperback) | ISBN 9780593083468 (ebook)
Subjects: LCSH: New business enterprises. | Strategic planning. | Problem solving.
Classification: LCC HD62.5 .B4548 2021 (print) | LCC HD62.5 (ebook) | DDC 658.1/1—dc23
LC record available at https://lccn.loc.gov/2020034366

LC ebook record available at https://lccn.loc.gov/2020034367

Printed in the United States of America
1st Printing

Book design by Alaina Sullivan

This book is dedicated to my abuelita, mami, and my tias—the strong Mexican women who raised and taught me to show up, never give up, and fight for what's right.

And to all the dreamers, doers, and hustlers out there. Anything is possible and everything is worth it.

Contents

START BEFORE YOU STOP

➡️ "Hey, there's a girl, she's going to make us some aprons for the restaurant," said Chef Josef, the head chef at Bäco Mercat in LA. "Do you want to buy one?"

Everything froze. I was a cook in Chef Josef's kitchen, and I didn't know this apron supplier, but I knew I did *not* want one of her aprons.

Oh my God. Do I say something about my apron company? I mean, it's not really a company yet, but it WILL be. My aprons are going to make everyone who wears them feel like they matter. They'll make them feel like the amazing cooks and artists and makers that they are. We all hate wearing these cheap, shitty, scratchy aprons that fit about as well as a hospital gown. This is my chance. The opportunity boat is sailing by. I have to get on it!

"Chef, *I* have an apron company!!" I said, taking a little liberty with the verb tense. "I will make you those aprons."

"What are you talking about?" Chef Josef said, giving me his steady, inquisitive look that I knew so well. "You're a line cook in my kitchen."

It was a fair point. I *was* a line cook in his kitchen, standing at my station, chopping vegetables.

"I have an apron company, Chef. I started it recently. I would love to make you those aprons. I can totally do it. What is she charging you? What is she making them out of? What's her turnaround? I can do it faster . . . and better."

"She said it's gonna take six weeks."

I could tell by his tone that he was not too jazzed about that timeline.

"I'll do it in four," I said.

"Yeah?" he said.

"Yeah, for real," I said. "I've already been working on it!" Well, I'd been talking to my coworker Kevin about it, and I actually had just filed for a DBA, or Doing Business As, which is the very first step in registering a company. So it felt real enough, at least to me. But as for a "company," that was pretty much all in my head. I didn't have a design. I didn't have a pattern. I didn't have fabric. I didn't know where to buy fabric. I certainly didn't know how to run a company, nor did I have the infrastructure, or even know anyone with a sewing machine, yet. I had no idea how long it would take to do any of this, let alone *all* of it. But I was damn well going to try. And I was gonna get it done.

"OK, alright, cool," Chef said.

WTF? Really?

If I screwed up the aprons, I'd probably lose my job. Not to mention that I respected Chef Josef to the moon and back, and I didn't want to mess this up. I could not let him down, with an all-caps NOT. At the end of the night, I clocked out and called Kevin to tell him that we had a 40-unit order—even though our last conversation had been about early days decisions, like finding fabrics and a pattern, and what we'd call the company.

My dream to make aprons had sprung from an observation of this *thing* that would happen at the end of a shift: the kitchen staff would change out of their work uniforms and come back in to grab their stuff, looking and carrying themselves like totally different humans. In their civvies (civilian clothes) after work, or when I ran into them at the farmers' market on Sundays, they looked like real people with *way* more pep in their step and just generally more at ease. (And by "they" I mean "we.") Because in our standard-issue aprons, which were either rented from a linen service, or bought as cheaply as possible, we looked like we didn't matter. They were all but made of flimsy paper masquerading as fabric. They were so basic they often didn't adjust around the neck, or have a useful pocket, for our tweezers, pens, or sharpies. Or, if they did, they tore off with the slightest tug. At the night's end, we tossed them aside, the feeling of disposability still clinging to us. And that had to change. *Does everyone in the kitchen feel so shitty before they look so shitty? What if they had a uniform that didn't make them feel like cogs in a wheel?*

In between slamming out orders on the line, Kevin and I would brainstorm ideas, which I'd jot down and stuff into my recipe book, right next to my cooking notes.

For inspiration, all I had to do was to look down at my own mangled apron. My pockets always got caught on the handles of the lowboy refrigerators and ripped off, with the floppy fabric left dangling. In between orders, I'd draw a sketch for a new style of pocket that had reinforced corners to stand up to the mayhem of kitchen work.

"OK, what do you think about this apron?" I'd ask Kevin. We'd have a quick exchange while he cooked up the Wagyu beef or whatever protein he was responsible for that night, and then, like a hummingbird, I'd flit back over to my kitchen station. He was much more introspective and liked to analyze everything, so between us, we created a good balance.

Once again, however, Kevin and I had no plan, no supplies, and no manufacturing process. Now we had four weeks to get all of those things. Under these circumstances, I could have easily fallen into two states of disaster:

I could have been so lost about how to proceed next that I ducked my head into my turtle shell and waited for it all to go away. *What have I gotten myself into?! I don't know if I can do this. This seems nuts.*

I could have tried to plan out every single detail of this company before moving forward with this process, and overanalyzed every step we had to take, so that the entire production turned into a tangled mess of missed due dates and failed plans.

INSTEAD, I CHOSE PROGRESS over perfection and went with a method that had always carried me through before: Decide to do it. Try. Fail. Learn. Hustle. Go try again. And keep going, relentlessly. From an early age, I'd been leaping off mini-precipices without looking down, from repainting almost every room in my mom's house, while she was at work, and without permission (which she later told me, calmly and quietly, was "nice"), to taking over the

RESILIENCE

=

WAR
WOUNDS

+

STAMINA

family finances as a completely green high schooler, because my single mom was stressed about money. (I figured out checkbooks and budgeting along the way.)

Not that I always stuck the landings. Far from it. As I'd already learned, mistakes are quite literally unavoidable, especially when you're running fast. But I realized that as long as I was in motion, and in action mode, I'd figure it out, eventually.

OK, what are the elements that we need to make aprons?

Well, we needed a pattern, fabric, sewers. And to lasso any of that, we needed money and the bones of a plan. I was making $10 an hour as a line cook (minimum wage back then), so I wasn't earning quite enough to fund a whole manufacturing venture. I asked Chef Josef for a deposit and he agreed to pay me half up front, which was around $750. We supplemented that nest egg with $500. It still wasn't much to launch a company. I didn't even own a sewing machine (or know how to use one). But I knew what I wanted to make and roughly how I wanted them to be. Now, we needed some helping hands. And we needed them yesterday.

Kevin thought to introduce me to his friend, another Kevin. Kevin Carney owned the design/retail business Mohawk General Store. It quickly became clear that he had the know-how to make a pattern—hooray! I didn't know how much he'd charge, but I had a sense that it was more than we could afford. So, I thought about what I had to offer in exchange, instead of money: *Well, I work as a private chef, and I'm a line cook at Bäco Mercat, and at Providence, and that's a two Michelin star restaurant, and people love a good*

When pursuing a dream, it's OK to be a little shameless when trying, when being scrappy, and when showing up! Never for a second let anyone make you feel ashamed for trying to make something out of your life. Leave your shyness at the door, along with your fear of "What if they say no?" And forget the people who already did say no.

meal. *What if I barter food and meals for the things I need for us to get this company off the ground?*

"I cook at Providence, which is fancy, so . . . ," I said to Mohawk General Kevin. "I'm going to make you food, and you make me that pattern. Deal?"

With his raised eyebrows radiating skepticism, but also curiosity, Mohawk General Kevin agreed. Sure, he probably thought I was a bit crazy and a lot desperate, but as long as I got my pattern, I didn't mind. I had an order to fill!

As he sat in my divey kitchen, with my roommates passing by, I made Mohawk General Kevin a simple but beautiful omelet and salad. He was very agile with his pattern-making skills, holding the paper up to the light, trimming it here, editing it there, making it longer. And before I knew what had happened, the pattern was ready.

From there, Mohawk General Kevin put us in touch with someone who knew a shoemaker, who had a guy who'd cut leather for him once. My Spanish came in handy. He invited us to his "studio," located in a cul-de-sac full of old beat-up cars, random dogs running in the street, and what looked like a triplex in total disrepair. It was a low-key sewing facility being run out of someone's home. He was an old-school *schmatta* (Yiddish slang for rag seller/someone in the garment industry)—weathered by life but rife with experience. Plus, he had a guy, Jose, who was available to sew for us. We immediately struck a deal, and I gave him the pattern and the sample fabric we'd picked out and brought him. He was a pro. And he put up with the fact that we were so not.

When we got our first sample and tried it on a few days later, our not-pro-ness really showed—there were boobs and hips hanging out everywhere. So we tweaked the pattern. Got the new sample. Now, it wasn't landing right at the knee. And it puckered. So, we shaved an inch from the back. Tweak. Adjust. Improve.

Getting the fabric right took almost as many tries. We didn't know about pre-shrinking, or qualities, weights, or origins (sooo many details). So, Kevin took all twenty-nine yards of continual fabric—what we had thought was premium denim—to the laundromat. He washed it, dried it. Only, it didn't look quite right. Then he and I set up two ironing boards, end to end, trying to iron out the wrinkles, which were so severe, they seemed like they were permanent. When that failed, we had to buy the fabric again. Start over from the beginning.

And yet, somehow, we came out on the other side, aprons in hand, because there was no time to analyze the errors or fix our process—we just needed to get it done, and fast.

I delivered our order to Chef Josef. On time. Hallelujah! It was so exciting!

The aprons were ironed and stacked up as neatly as sticks of gum in a Doublemint pack. I was beaming with pride. The best part about it was, when the cooks put on their aprons, they literally lifted their heads up higher and looked prouder. They were happy to have

▲ With Chef Josef and the Bäco Mercat crew in our first aprons

better gear, but more than anything, I think they were happy some-one had thought about them and all the details that went into mak-ing something functional and beautiful for the job they were doing.

• • •

THIS WAS THE UNLIKELY BEGINNING of my multimillion-dollar company, and a major turning point in my path to being a real entrepreneur. I attribute the success to a lot of grit, luck, help from many, but most important, my willingness to try. We spend too much time planning, judging, and deciding it can't be done, and not enough time embracing those wild ideas and pushing through the impossible to see them come to life. That's the journey. And I wrote this book to show you how it's possible.

Inspired by my two cultures and upbringings, I named my company Hedley & Bennett. First, after Hedley Bennett, my En-glish grandfather, a mechanical engineer and proper rocket scien-tist, who was a highly analytical sort. Plus, Bennett was what Chef (Cimarusti) had nicknamed me in the kitchen, which, to me, repre-sented my Latin side and upbringing—a little more spunk and col-or. From the beginning, every aspect of H&B was meant to express where I came from and what I wanted to share with others, connect-ing people one apron at a time, and growing out into the universe from there.

Our gear is now worn around the world, in thousands of restau-rants, and by countless home cooks. I set out to make the best apron ever, but really, I changed the way employers treat a set of modern-day blue-collar workers—and the way kitchen staff look and feel. And after so many years of collaborating with chefs on the front lines, our aprons are like a bridge from the professional kitchen to the home kitchen, because no matter who you are, when you rock H&B, you're a proper cook, and the world should be your oyster. That original idea has become the foundation for a community of thousands who wear the H&B logo on their chest, loudly and proudly. It's much more than a uniform. It's an attitude.

In the pages ahead, you'll find the story of how I created my company, leading with my dream and figuring out the details from there. It's also a story about how I took big leaps, and why you should take chances too. Whether you're starting a business, launching a personal project, working up the nerve to pitch your boss a crazy idea, or just trying to quit the damn procrastinating and live life more boldly, you can use this book as inspiration and motivation to get out of your head and into action. We ALL have that entrepreneurial spark within us, and we ARE CAPABLE of being the change we want to see around us, so stop just wondering, and start exploding things into reality.

The truth is, you can say yes to things you have no idea how to execute and then use your creative problem-solving power—and heart and guts—to conquer the shit storms as they come.

I could have easily tabled my idea for a time when I had less on my plate. I was already working three jobs—I definitely didn't need a fourth project! And not just any project, but one as the founder

I Had

- ☐ A purpose, a North Star
- ☐ Chutzpah

- ☐ Stick-to-itiveness
- ☐ Grit

- ☐ DBA (Doing Business As)
- ☐ Three jobs

- ☐ A noggin for problem solving
- ☐ $500 savings

- ☐ A strong Mexican mom, abuelita, and tias who got it done, despite zero resources growing up

- ☐ Two chefs who gave me a chance and a leg up into a tight-knit community: Chef Josef Centeno taught me grit; Chef Cimarusti, attention to detail and perfection.

- ☐ Humble enthusiasm
- ☐ A willingness to fail

- ☐ Being my own cheerleader
- ☐ My chef community

- ☐ The courage to stare errors in the eye

I Didn't Have

☑ A four-year college degree

☑ Business plan   ☑ MBA

☑ Money   ☑ Trust fund

☑ Loan

☑ Investors

☑ Experience designing or manufacturing garments

☑ Experience working at a traditional company

☑ Cofounder (Kevin helped me to launch, but a few months in, I was on my own)

> **What you have trumps what you don't, and sometimes what might seem like a deficit is actually an asset.**

and person solely responsible for a company I was making up as I went along. But if I'd waited until I had all my ducks in a row, I would have never done it.

When turning your dream into reality—to break outside of the comfort zone of your usual audience or channel—your first major roadblock is the voice in your head telling you you're not quuiiite ready.

Some people say that success happens when preparation meets opportunity. A more helpful piece of advice is that you are never prepared. Not FULLY prepared, anyway. There will always be a few doubts rattling around in there.

Before any real-life obstacles come crashing into you—and they will—you'll have to bushwhack your way through your own forest of doubts and reservations. These doubts masquerade as rational, but they're more likely coming from a place of fear.

But you gotta leap anyhow. Starting before you're perfectly ready is the best way to learn, edit, adjust, and improve your concept. We didn't know our pattern needed to be tweaked—or our fabric, or our straps—until we made a sample. We figured it out and learned as we went. It didn't feel good, but it also didn't kill my company. Turned out, me and my mini-staff could survive a whole lot more than we thought, and the bumps in the road weren't just a part of the road—they were a part of the damn journey AND the way forward.

That survival guide for falling on your ass and getting back up again is included in the pages to come, too.

I know that it's not easy to cannonball into the unknown of following your dream. Maybe your dream is still a hunch, a seed of an idea that just occurred to you. Maybe it's so different that you haven't shared it with anyone yet, afraid of what they'll say, think, or feel about it. Or maybe this dream has been years in the making. You've utilized countless journals to document your noodling, you've read piles of inspirational books, and you've thought through everything that could possibly go right and wrong. And yet, here you sit, still frozen.

If any of this describes you, then I'm glad you're here. You've found me, the dream first, details later maniac. This isn't just how I think. It's who I am as a person. It's practically in my DNA. For better and for worse. I'm stuck with me, and all of my madcap desires to make things happen, despite the risk. Like cutting through the forest with a machete, you have to pioneer your own way—no one has gone before you to clear the path. So stop just imagining the adventure, and fling yourself out into the ocean of life. Let's do this!

How to Embark on a

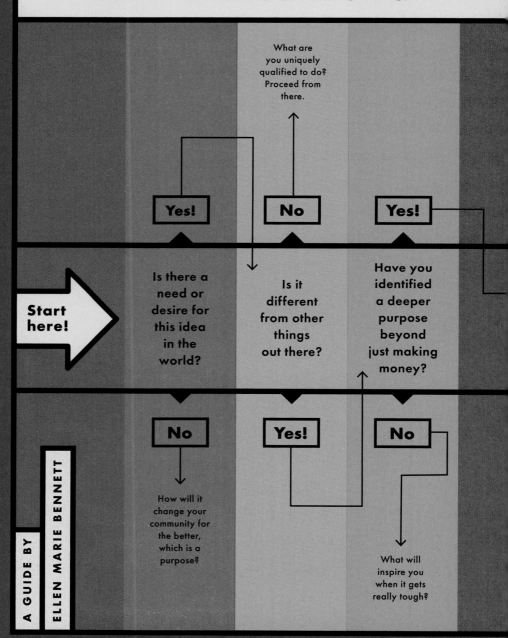

What are you uniquely qualified to do? Proceed from there.

Yes!

No

Yes!

Start here!

Is there a need or desire for this idea in the world?

Is it different from other things out there?

Have you identified a deeper purpose beyond just making money?

No

Yes!

No

How will it change your community for the better, which is a purpose?

What will inspire you when it gets really tough?

A GUIDE BY ELLEN MARIE BENNETT

Lifechanging Journey

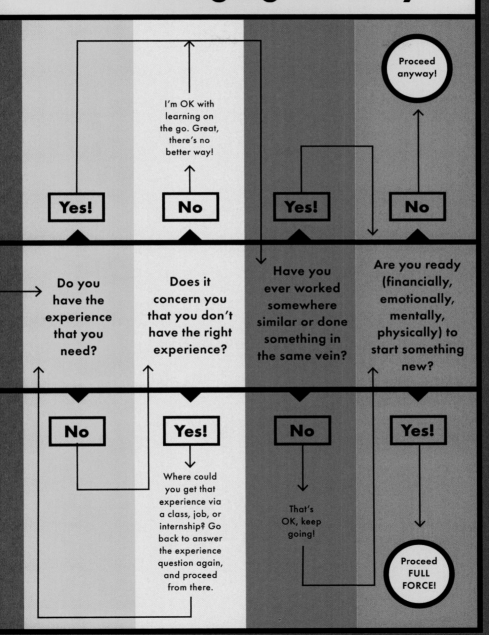

1

CRASH & LEARN

➡ "Bennett!" Chef yelled at me a few nights after I'd proudly presented him with our first ever apron order.

"These aprons suck! The straps keep falling down, what the fuck?"

Oh shit shit sheeeeeet. I was usually a Ping-Pong ball, leaping from my station to the six burners behind me, over to the nearby walk-in, and to the dish pit in the prep area. But I screeched to a halt. The busy Bäco kitchen seemed to freeze right along with me.

This was my first customer, my first opportunity, and I had somehow just ruined it.

My palms began to sweat. A string of "fuck, shit, crap" flooded my brain. I looked over at the other cook next to me, who looked back at me with wide, nervous eyes.

I hustled over to Chef Josef, calling out "behind," as I shot past cooks in the prep area to get to his office. I stood there, shaking in my clogs, and heard him out. I evaluated the damage. I stared at the damn aprons, starting with the one I was wearing. Even more important, for the rest of my shift, I observed them while they were in use by real cooks, including myself, in an actual professional kitchen. Yep, their flaws were obvious. He was right.

● ● ●

CHEF JOSEF'S OPINION meant everything to me—as a mentor and as a boss—and now he was unhappy with me, my product, and my company. Even the sous chef, Andy, who *loved* his apron, had proudly showed me how he'd used a fanny pack clip to gather the fabric in the back and make it hang right. I could tell he was happy just to have an upgraded apron, but I was supposed to be the one getting the design right. Not him. After thinking I'd pulled off a slam dunk, the emotional whiplash set in: *Maybe we were in over our heads. Was it wrong to have tried? Gah, I fucked this up . . .*

But no, hold on . . . I could fix this. *You cannot fucking give up— you're literally just getting started!!!!*

I took a deep breath and told Chef Josef in a calm, somewhat put together voice, "Chef, I totally hear you and you're absolutely

6 Things That Were Wrong with My First Apron Order

- The straps weren't effective, fell down every 5 seconds, and couldn't be adjusted properly.

- Even though they looked good as a whole, upon closer analysis, they had not been trimmed well (to remove the excess threads from the sewing process).

- There was no consistency in the aprons and certain pockets were ever so slightly angled, versus perfectly symmetrical.

- The pockets weren't strong enough to stand up to the abuse of line cooks—they needed to be reinforced.

- Even after our laundromat adventures, the fabric hadn't been properly prewashed and wrinkled more than it should have, plus it hadn't been tested, so it bled a little.

- The straps, which were supposed to lay flat, folded up on each other when you washed them.

right. These need to be better. Here's what I can do. Give me back half the aprons, so the team can still use half of them in service. I'll repair them in chunks and make them right. Once the first half is fixed, I'll bring them back and we can hand them out again, and then, I'll repair the other half. And thank you for all your honest feedback. I will take care of this."

With a small but firm smile, I walked out. I felt the same fire in my belly that flared up when I got my first order.

I had a narrow window of time to get this right, and I couldn't sleep on it, so I grabbed the little money we'd made from that order, which amounted to a few hundred dollars, after we'd bought the fabric twice, and paid our sewer. I stocked up on supplies for Chef's next batch of aprons. In theory, the first aprons had been right, visually, but now, I actually had real feedback, and a focus group of sorts, telling me how my product was wrong. There seemed to be a silver lining here, if I could get them right—but how?

I gave myself a pep talk: *I'm driving the car now, and along the way, I'm going to have to drive through some bumpy ass roads, so HANDS ON THE WHEEL, BENNETT.*

With all this new context I'd been given, I went back to the fabric store where we'd gotten our first material and spent hours and hours going through all of the different possibilities, touching everything, getting my face right up close to each different weave, weighing the pros and cons, even when the difference was sometimes so minuscule, it was nearly imperceptible. But I knew that this was the only way to find my solution. And, eventually, I did. In

When facing an overwhelming problem, do a whiteboard or paper brainstorm and scribble down all the ways you think you can fix it. Get yourself in a solution-oriented mindset and don't even think for a second: Woe is me. How could this happen? Instead, realize that you are in the driver's seat and ask yourself what you can do to put things right. And then, get to work!

the end, I bought a premium denim that was thicker, more durable, and washed more nicely—so it didn't wrinkle, and it hung better.

When it came time to rethink the straps, I brought this same intense laser focus to bear on my problem-solving process. I didn't just get more of the red twill tape we'd used for our first straps. This time, I was absolutely going to get it right. I found this place called Trims 4 Less. It was on the edge of downtown LA, in an industrial neighborhood called Vernon I'd never been to before. It felt so far from the city I knew that it was almost as if it was on Mars. (Ironically, it's near where the H&B HQ is today—more about that later.)

This was literally a wonderland of every kind of possible trim and accent and cord you could possibly want (and a bunch of stuff so esoteric and specific, you'd probably never think to want it, such as rickrack, pom-poms, and metallic trims). The bolts of trim rose twelve-feet-high toward the ceiling. They had maybe a hundred different webbings, with every variety of thickness and density. I scoured the place, snipping off small samples, holding them in my hands, pulling on them, letting them lie flat, and trying to envision what would make for the best possible strap.

Even after all of that, I still didn't find my perfect webbing there. That would have to wait for another day. But I did stumble upon this amazing brass hardware that had a classic, timeless look to it, and which ended up becoming a part of the strap we use to this day.

During my strap reconnaissance, I also made a point of introducing myself to the owner of the shop. As I suspected, we went on to do tons of business together over the years, and ended up becoming friends. As opportunities arise to form relationships, take them! That's really what it's all about in the long run anyway.

My first customers turned into some of my most special relationships. Chef Josef, for instance, gave me a safe space to experiment. He didn't assume I would fail. He assumed I would get it right. So, I used Chef and my fellow line cooks as guinea pigs, registering how and why their aprons didn't work for them during service. We were jammed together in a tiny space, and it was easy for me to get their feedback on the fly, sort of like a super-casual, on-the-ground market research session (with more swearing). I went back to my little recipe book where I'd hoarded all of my notes. Truth time: If I wanted to be a long-term business owner, I needed to play the long game with my customers and my material choices. Here's some of the quick improvements that happened in that week:

- ☐ **Pre-testing my fabrics**
- ☐ **Changing to double needle stitching on the corners of every pocket, to protect them from ripping off**
- ☐ **Rethinking the strap, again and again and again (the most important tweak we made)**

We must've created ten or twelve different straps in a few days. I whipped through prototype after prototype, testing my design every step of the way. The trick, of course, was that people came in all different shapes and sizes. Until I figured out how to make my aprons actually fit each and every one of them like a glove, they'd never get the confidence boost and feeling I was aiming for with my original apron epiphany. The strap was one of my secret weapons. I just had to figure out the best way to employ it.

After two weeks that felt like two years, we developed the Hedley & Bennett strap system that we use to this day. And we did it with no wiggle room to get it wrong. We needed a solution. Now. The new strap wasn't just the poly-cotton shoestring of other standard-issue aprons. And it wasn't the twill tape of our first iteration, which I could now see was honestly not very good. I had finally found my perfect webbing. It was 100 percent cotton, American-made, beautiful, durable, and, most important, FUNCTIONAL! It felt better against the skin of the chef wearing it. I'd come up with a new approach—an adjustable strap. Along with that perfect brass slider I'd nosed my way into, it was now a bulletproof strap design—indestructible and perfectly sized for everybody. Plus, I could dye it. That meant I could change it to be on-brand for different restaurants. It wasn't a quick fix—it was a path forward.

You may be thinking, well, great, but you could've saved yourself all that anxiety and unpleasantness if you'd just tested your designs before delivering the first batch. But here's the thing. Putting your idea out in the world is the most efficient way to fine-tune your concept. Kevin and I were just two people, with our particular heights and body types. And while we did try on the aprons in my apartment, we weren't really seeing them in their natural habitat, with all of its added stresses and splatters. It wasn't until we actually released our first apron into the wild that we got the kind of honest feedback about how it fell short, from which we could build the better apron that didn't. In order to go through this generative process, we had to accept the ego bruising and downright terror that went along with fucking up the first time. There was no simulation that could have given us the same information. Or the same pressure to find a true solution, not just a quick fix. So, as uncomfortable as it was, we did things exactly right.

If foresight was 20/20—if I could read the future, in other words—I would've done a bunch of things differently during the first few years of H&B's existence. But what I wouldn't have changed was this . . . TRYING. I know, it can be nerve-wracking. Courage means doing it anyway. The cold hard truth is that you don't know until you know sometimes.

When you test drive an idea, functioning with incomplete information is a given. The mistakes and failures—and the successes—are the one-way road to getting that information. To come out on the other side, it's going to require listening, editing, and adjusting quickly when new information comes in. Otherwise, you'll be caught in a closed loop of fear forever. That's why I never linger too long on the planning stage. I'm always happiest as soon as I start getting my hands dirty.

When you put yourself and your dream into the world, you need to have a brutally honest sounding board to tell you what is and isn't working, like I had with Chef Josef and the other cooks in the Bäco kitchen. Separate the personal and emotional from the professional, and lap up every opportunity to improve. Because if you're not willing to get better, then why bother?

As it turned out, I didn't need to nail the first batch for H&B to survive. All I needed to do was start. Sure, any profit we had earned was completely gone. But I didn't care. As Uncle Ted, a successful businessman and one of my first mentors, always said: "Your word is worth solid gold." So, when it came down to it, my mantra was: *Chef Josef is my one and only customer. We cannot fuck this up. We must make this right.* And we did.

Diamonds are made under pressure, right?

How to Enlist People's Help in Testing Your Ideas

➤ This is just how I did it, not the only way. But I can tell you this approach has worked wonders for me, and not just for perfecting my aprons, but also for building relationships that have led to the ironclad apron squad we have today.

■ Go in person. If you can't, call. Or email. Or text. Or send an Instagram direct message. Make contact. With as much face time as possible.

_____

☐ Don't be afraid to ask in the first place.

_____

■ Be curious, not defensive.

_____

■ Show appreciation for all input, even the negative or off-point.

_____

☐ When people seem unsure, try to help them home-in on what they actually think.

_____

■ Don't just show the "before." Show the "after"— how feedback has been employed.

_____

2

The First Scary Thing

➡ Maybe we should rewind a little.

If you need confidence to try, confidence to examine your failures honestly, and confidence to try again—and if, like lots of people, you're not bold by nature—then how exactly do you find that confidence? How the hell do you scrunch up your eyes and leap into the unknown? We're just told to "be confident," but no one tells us where to GET IT.

Confidence, I've found, is like a savings fund that you invest in over years and decades. Every time I do something scary and witness myself come out alive and still kicking, despite the shit storms along the way, I'm making a deposit, and my account balance grows.

I call this my confidence belt. I made the first notches on my belt before I understood the long game—but I did notice from the start that it felt pretty damn good to practice being brave. I also found that it didn't take much to grow my self-reliance. I'm not saying you've got to run with the bulls or go skydiving. Just tackling something you've never done before—a little, scary thing—and pulling it off (even imperfectly), is all it takes to scratch out a well-earned notch. And from there, it gets easier to triumph over the big things that go into making dreams happen.

When I was in high school in Glendale, just north of Los Angeles, I was surrounded by kids from rich families who were superstars in the making. I knew they'd grow up to be models and actors, and they did, too. Then there was me, this strange kid with a frizzy, curly, triangle-shaped head of hair that got me docked with the nickname Cavewoman. My parents were divorced. We had almost no money for anything. My dad was thousands of miles away. My mom, the cutest, five-foot-one Mexican mama, worked long hours as a registered nurse, and I was home alone, all the time, with my little sister, Melany. At first, I tried to fit in and find my slot in the crayon box of school. I tried to be the yellow crayon, alongside the kids who were red, and blue. I really did. But in no world could I hide the fact that I talked too loud and too fast and that I cared about things other kids didn't—like painting almost our entire apartment, balancing the family checkbook, and trying out new recipes. And as anyone who remembers what it's like to fight for survival in the teenage Thunderdome knows, not fitting in is deeply painful.

But since being an outsider meant I had nothing to lose, it lit a fire in me that pushed me down a different path than my peers. After a little while, when I realized my attempts to jam myself into the Crayola set weren't working anyhow, I didn't even try to fit in. Instead, I dashed to the end of my alternative high school program, then bopped around LA, nannying, juggling a bunch of random odd jobs, and dating a guy my mom was sure was too old for me.

(He probably was.) I couldn't afford the college I wanted to go to, and I wasn't sure what I would study anyway.

Sometimes I felt like everyone had a plan but me. But somewhere deep inside, I felt my first little squirm of knowledge that there was something way bigger I was meant to be doing—or at least something very different—I just had no idea what it was.

The closest I had to an inkling of a path forward was my clear love for food. When I fed people, their faces lit up, and their whole selves smiled. Growing up, I spent my summers at my abuelita's house in Mexico, and I'd pass countless hours busy in the kitchen with her, where I threw down question after question: "What's in those tamales? What did you put in this stew? Can you show me?" Back home in Glendale, my mom was too busy working to make much more than reheated enchiladas and burritos from Trader Joe's. Meanwhile, the only foods my younger sister Melany would eat for the longest time were grilled cheese and poppy seed bread, dipped in milk—what a combo.

My first properly successful culinary conquest was at age twelve, when I re-created the spicy, meaty picadillo I found simmering on my friend's mom's front burner one afternoon. The smell immediately brought me back to my abuelita's house, where she'd make the same dish. I lifted lids, smelling things, clattering them back down, and pestering my friend's mom with questions. She listed the main ingredients merrily: ground beef, tomatoes, onions, potatoes, carrots, if you're feeling it, corn—and so on and so forth. The next morning, I launched myself out of bed, propelled by my plan for the day.

I didn't bother asking my mom for permission, because she was always working and expected me to make the right decisions for Melany and me anyway. She trusted me, and that meant a lot to me. I bribed Melany with the promise of a snack and lugged her six long blocks over to our local grocery store, where, using the debit card with my name on it that I'd somehow convinced Bank of America to issue me at fifteen, I got the necessary ingredients. I pushed the shopping cart all the way home, Melany riding inside.

As I mixed in a little of this, a dash of that, I tried not to think about the fact that our monthly grocery budget could be in the red if I wasted expensive ingredients. I waited anxiously to see whether I could coax this pile of mush into that recipe I'd smelled the day before. Soon, though with the grease popping from the pan and the chilies making my eyes water, I knew I was on the right track. My hands busy, pulling the ingredients together into something so much better than their parts, I got one of my first tastes of creative euphoria.

But the real victory came later that evening when my mother came home. She walked in the front door in her scrubs, just as always, already preoccupied with other tasks ahead of her. But as she walked into the kitchen and saw and smelled what I'd prepared, she stopped for a rare, quick moment. "Thank you, Mami," she said, happiness broadcasting across her face. (In my Latin family, like a lot of Latin families, all the ladies call their kids Mami. I was Mami. My mom was Mami, and so on.)

OK, so she still had to deal with a few work calls before she was free to eat. But then she heated a tortilla, the smell of toasted corn filling the kitchen, and she actually sat down to enjoy a hot meal. It was one of the first notches on my confidence belt. *Aha! I did it!* Head held up high, alone in our kitchen in Glendale, I got it for the first time: BE YOUR OWN CHEERLEADER. When you believe in yourself, anything and everything is possible.

So culinary school, right? I'd looked at the CIA (Culinary Institute of America) and Le Cordon Bleu, but going there cost $30,000 to $70,000. There was no way in hell. My family didn't have that kind of money. And although I could handle a "no" from other people, hearing a "no" from my parents was like getting punched in the face of my mind. I wasn't going to go to regular college. I didn't want to be a nanny forever. I was truly at a crossroads, with no clear marching orders. So I figured some change of scenery might help. *Go explore, Ellen. It will help. It has to.*

So at nineteen years old, I decided to move to Mexico City, Mexico—by myself. Even though I had family in Mexico and had been spending big chunks of time there since I was a little kid, we didn't have any relatives in Mexico City. It was more like we knew somebody who knew somebody there. This was back in 2006, before Mexico City became a popular tourist spot, like it has in recent years. Mexico was NOT cool yet, not safe, and not a smart place for a teenager to move ALONE, at least according to friends and their parents.

I bought a plane ticket. One way.

THE FIRST SCARY THING

● ● ●

WHEN I TOUCHED DOWN, I wasn't necessarily planning to stay for more than a month or two, so I just had one tall suitcase and my backpack and a purse. I took my luggage straight to my rented room in the Roma Norte neighborhood. And waltzed right into my new reality: one small room with bunk beds that were rusty and creaky; a strange mini-dresser, and a window overlooking the noisiest, most crowded sea of buildings I had ever seen in my life. The floor had obviously been redone a dozen times and still looked worn. The kitchen and bathroom were tiny and super basic—the kitchen was in a closet, essentially. There was only enough hot water to shower sometimes. I was renting a corner of the apartment, along with four other girls who'd come from around the world to study and work in Mexico City. They were all nice, but my landing was far from a slam dunk. There were plenty of nights during my first week in the city when I tossed and turned, thinking, *What the hell am I doing here?*

Luckily, I'd been speaking Spanish my whole life, so I was pretty much fluent. The first thing I noticed was that people were more likely to linger and joke as they handed me back my change or held the door for me. *Damn. This is way different.* That high-octane, steam engine approach to life I'd inherited from my abuelita, while all of the other kids my age were laid-back and cool, was the new norm. I looked around me in Mexico City, and everyone was just zestier. They were friendly. They were loud. They hugged and kissed people. And it was completely OK!! And then, I had this epiphany:

The Flavors of Doubt

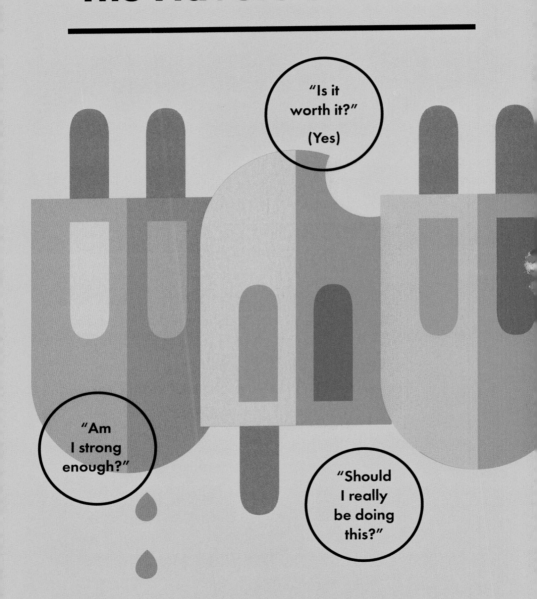

➤ Like a box of popsicles, there are a rainbow of possible nagging fears and insecurities you might encounter whenever you start something new:

"Oh my God. I belong here. I'm Mexican!" For once, it wasn't me who felt different, after years of being my school's resident outcast. *This is way BETTER.* The pace and the rhythm of the city made sense to me. Before long, I felt like I'd found my people. Finally, I realized how much my Mexican culture had always been in me. Finally, I'd found my home.

That's when it occurred to me: *I should actually stay here. I should make it official.* With the memories of my recent successes playing on a loop in my head—buying the damn plane ticket, showing up, renting a room, securing groceries, and making a few friends—I figured I could try to get a job.

I'm glad I didn't know how hard THAT would be when I started. I was up against cultural barriers, a scant résumé, the painfully difficult process of becoming a Mexican citizen (which I wanted to do instead of getting a permit to work as a foreigner), not to mention the agonizingly difficult process of becoming an adult, just to name a few obstacles.

● ● ●

AS THE MONTHS PASSED and my confidence belt became slashed with hard-earned notches, I found myself doing things I'd thought were way out of my league. A new friend who worked as a model suggested I go to see her agents, because I'd told her I needed a job. So I set up an appointment. And holy shazam! Then another, and another, and within two months of arriving, I had THREE talent

4 Hard Things I Did in the Coming Months

☐

Getting my Mexican citizenship was a four-month process. First: rent an apartment, put a utility bill in my name, and get a Mexican ID, for which I needed a Mexican passport. That required a ninety-minute flight and a seven-plus-hour car trip to get a copy of my mom's birth certificate. Then, I navigated a bureaucratic maze that involved several in-person office visits and getting a post office ID that, for no clear reason, required a black and white photo. Crash course on life in Mexico!

☐

I rented the most amazing apartment in Roma Norte, with this cool black and white checkerboard lobby. Only, I couldn't afford it. So, way before Airbnb, I rented rooms to students and people like me, who were visiting Mexico City and needed a place to stay. I even turned the living room into an extra bedroom to earn some additional bucks, which helped me to not only cover my own rent completely, but also to make a little extra cash. Bonus!

☐

I enrolled in a Mexican culinary school. It was WAY cheaper than American options, but still just as good, a fact I used to get my dad to help me pay for it. But I still had to take a bus and a subway to get there (no car), and my classes were in Spanish. Let's just say, this included some specialized lingo and was a crash course in proper Spanish, not just the conversational Spanish I had grown up with.

☐

I got a job as a commercial actress, and booth babe for canola oil, armored vehicles, and the companies that sell the paint for the stripes on the highways. I got a second job on the Mexican NFL show (in a jersey). I got a third job, announcing the lottery on TV. Sometimes I made up jobs, like selling Christmas trees to get a deal at the biggest market in the city, then lugging my tree home on a bus. Sometimes I worked odd jobs, doing simultaneous translation for the Mexican Railroad Union, and as a soap opera guest star.

agents in Mexico City, where they didn't mind my being repped by multiple people. They'd send me out, all across the massive city, to try out for who knows what crazy opportunities were up for grabs—sometimes as many as four to six auditions in a single day.

Soon, I started acting in commercials. But commercials weren't everyday jobs, and out of every ten auditions, I got maybe two—if that. I needed to work more. So on one of my many days of auditions, I tried out for a job doing commentary on an American football show. When they heard how I could flip from fluent Spanish to perfect American English in the same light tone: "y aquí estamos con Tony ROMO!" I landed the job, which was every Sunday. Boom! Steady work! This was also on one of the country's biggest networks, TV Azteca, oh, and it was filmed live! Our two male announcers sat on a couch, discussing the highlights of the game as it was played live back in the States. Meanwhile, I stood on the other side of the set, by a vertical screen that showed clips, and added color commentary. Wearing white go-go boots, a miniskirt, a football jersey with "Ellen" on the back, and a mask of two hours of professionally applied makeup, I read from a teleprompter—in Spanish—and tried not to let any bad words slip in, which I did a few times—causing indigestion all around. My heart always felt like it was going to explode out of my chest. I was learning to hit my marks and read lines, live, in front of 3 to 4 million people. Plus, I hadn't known anything about football, which I was now getting a crash course in, while living in Mexico City, alone, renting rooms to strangers to make it all work, and simultaneously convincing my dad to cover the cost of school for me in a foreign country. TOTALLY NORMAL, nothing to see here, just a nineteen-year-old figuring it out.

The next stop on my wild job journey was becoming the lottery announcer on the same TV channel, which meant reading the numbers every weekday evening. Also great training for communicating—not just information, but also energy and enthusiasm—in front of a camera, and to millions of people. (Crazy sidenote: the woman who took the job after me got caught for being part of a studio-wide scam to try to fix the lottery and steal millions. Don't look at me—I stuck to the cue cards!)

I also discovered that I could get steady gigs as a "booth babe," aka someone selling other people's products at trade shows by helping to usher potential customers into the booth and talking to them about everything the brand offered—think door-to-door salesman, while standing in place. Hahaha. Now this might sound sultry, and yes, they did hire cute girls. But instead of wearing a bikini, I wore a suit, and I talked up every possible kind of business under the sun and the moon, from canola oil, cell phones, and armored cars to doctors' conventions and bank events. It was far from glamorous. I took the bus, then the subway, plus a "pesero" or minibus, then walked twenty minutes to get to the convention center. I could have gone in a taxi, but I was saving up all of my pesos. I worked my ass off, standing for eight to ten hours straight, in heels, selling to and being ignored by thousands of people, making friends out of strangers, walking in and out of the trade show, while also being checked out.

Mexico City Hustle

One-way ticket to Mexico

A Cook at a *fonda* (a small stand)

Trade Show "Booth Babe"

Cheerleader Host on American football show

Simultaneous Translator for Mexican railroad union

English Tutor (to a boss's son)

➤ Some of my many jobs while living in Mexico City

Airbnb-style Landlord (pre-Airbnb)

National Lottery Announcer on TV Azteca

Christmas Tree Saleswoman

Culinary School Student

TV Azteca Telenovela Trainee (acting, dancing, fencing, and on and on)

Leaving it all to go back to the US and start again to pursue my food career dreams

But I learned so much from this world and from watching all these trade show peeps in action—they were hustlers with a capital H. They all had a Nextel phone, a Blackberry, AND a cell phone, as if they were drug dealers of themselves. They'd be taking a call on one line while wrapping up a job, already negotiating for their next gig. And then, whoosh, they'd yank an impeccable fresh suit out of their bag, be changed in an instant, and on their way. They were always on time, always on point, and they made their customers feel important and special, never letting on that they were juggling dozens of clients. And they did all of this while making it look easy, but as I got to know them more, I realized these people had a fire in their bellies, and babies, kids, families who were solely dependent on them for making ends meet. Their conviction to get the job wasn't just for the thrill of it; their lives as single mothers, many times, depended on it. No one was there to save them if they fell down. It was a sight to see and an inspiration I'll never forget—fighting the good fight.

At this point, juggling so many jobs, I was now starting to make good money in Mexico, but still living scrappy, not to mention eating the best tacos of my life, once or twice a day. More important, I'd done the difficult groundwork of convincing the scared part of my brain—my inner little weird kid, maybe—that I could trust myself to take big jumps off the jagged cliffs of life.

When it comes to our dreams, most of us procrastinate for years, if not lifetimes, because it's scary as hell to admit you care about something and then go for it. Sure, I can tell you to just push through the fear and do the damn thing, but that's easier said than done. You can only bench-press so much angst. You have to prove to yourself that you can survive the uncomfortable, scary stuff. Next time you'll be able to do something even scarier.

• • •

YOU DON'T NEED TO journey to a foreign country. I chose that adventure because it was right for me at the time; I had always felt a close connection to my Mexican heritage and food, and I followed that unique path forward. What pulls you? What scares and excites you? Don't just give me the easy answer. Really dig deep. Down to that dream that maybe you've never even voiced inside your own head. And then, take the next step, even if it's just in private right now.

What are you so afraid of? That you'll ask someone for help, and they'll say no? Or laugh at you for trying? Are you concerned that your dignity and pride are at risk?

Yep, you probably are. And it probably is. But all the good stuff comes out of taking these kinds of risks.

I've had all of those fears. We all have. Proceed anyway. Those fears are just annoying little mosquitos of doubt, buzzing around you, on the path to your goal. Everyone encounters them. Keep marching forward anyway.

Find the courage to do the first scary thing: show up at the place where your dream begins. If that's too scary, call on the phone. Still too hard? Shoot off an email. Send a DM.

"DOUBT KILLS MORE DREAMS THAN FAILURE EVER WILL."

—Suzy Kassem

The first step should come from you. The world is not necessarily going to set your dream down in front of you with a nice shiny bow tied around it like a delicious fruit basket, and by the way, if it does, congrats to you. But you shouldn't let that gift make you feel entitled or complacent—keep earning that opportunity EVERY DAY. You went to a great college and got a perfect job, through the recommendation of a family friend. Good for you. Now what are you going to do with that position of power? What difference are you going to make to people around you in the world? Don't half-ass your dreams because you feel comfortable. Get comfortable being uncomfortable, and start making stuff happen around you.

> **When you get somewhere, head to the next somewhere, and never stop repeating the cycle. It's one thing to become successful. The next part is keeping it, maintaining it, and making it evolve.**

That right there has been the key to my journey.

The good news is, it doesn't all have to happen in one day. So, no matter your circumstances, figure out the right amount of chunks of your dream to bite off, and work on each until they're fully digested, and then, move on to the next. It'll get done. It really will.

Even better, with every step you take, you'll be getting stronger and surer of yourself. Confidence is a muscle that gets bigger the more you work it out, especially during your first few firestorms. Everything I'd taken on in my family's home life, my wild adventure in Mexico City, the three jobs I was juggling when I returned to LA, all gave me hard evidence that I could accomplish real tasks, even if I didn't start out knowing the first thing about how to do them. You can teach yourself confidence, too. It's as easy as daring yourself to do something, and then actually following through. It doesn't even matter if it turns out well or not—learning to deal with failure is part of the equation as well. As Winston Churchill famously said, "Never let a good crisis go to waste."

● ● ●

WHATEVER PATH YOU CHOOSE to build your confidence belt, it is crucial to find and cherish life accomplishments as you achieve them, no matter how small. I'm not talking about résumé building. I'm talking about doing things that feel good to you and build your self-confidence. These are the moments, big and small, when you realize, "Wow, I did something that I did not know I was capable of." Now mark those off on your belt and keep going.

Before you know it, you'll be ready to slip into white go-go boots, a miniskirt, and a football jersey with your name on the back, and talk to millions of people about a sport you don't know anything about.

6 Starter Ideas for Building Your Confidence Belt Based on Some Crazy-Ass Things I've Actually Tried, and Some Less Dramatic But Still Helpful Ways You Can Get Started

☑ Decide to leave the safety of your comfortable roost/ job/life and see what else is out there.

☑ Call someone you admire and (respectfully) ask them for advice or help in their area of expertise.

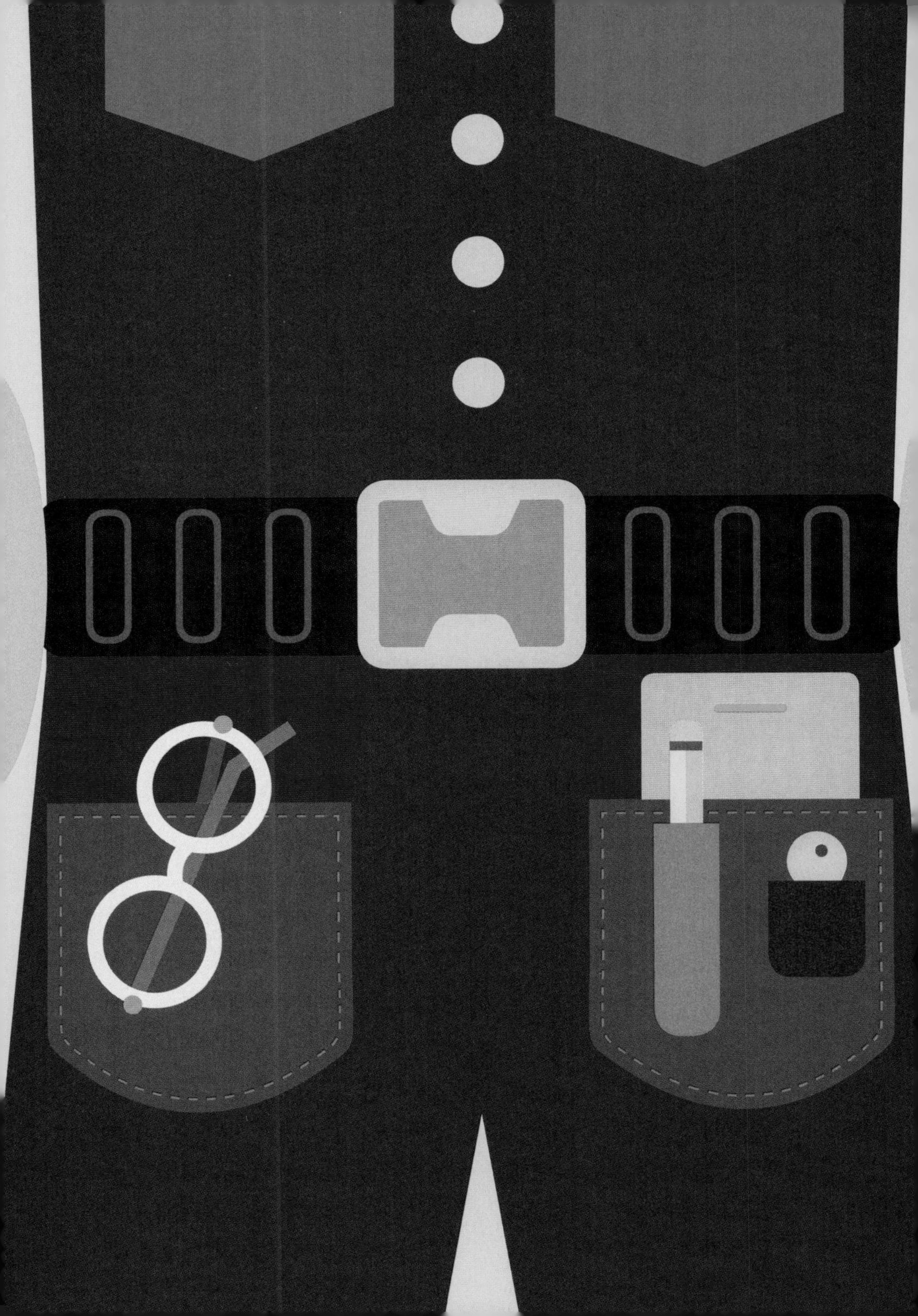

☐ Choose a mountain and climb it (this isn't a metaphor—I climbed Mt. Fuji by myself). I also trained for and ran a marathon. Maybe make that your personal challenge, or run a 3K, or do a sport that pushes you. You're not doing it for the activity itself, but for the resilience and tenacity it teaches you, and to prove to yourself that you can accomplish something big and hard.

☐ Get out of your comfort zone and barter your skills or services in exchange for learning something new.

☐ Take a class or listen to a podcast about a skill you've always wanted to learn. Do whatever you need to do to rise up out of your circumstances and prepare yourself with knowledge on how to deal with people, finances, communication, taxes, you name it. Take those hours you're currently on your phone and spend them reading instead—I promise you, you'll find you have more time than you think.

☐ Ask for the opportunity to intern somewhere challenging, where you have no experience. (In culinary school, I did what's called "staging"— pronounced "staahj-ing," which is kind of a cooking world version of interning or apprenticing— in a restaurant kitchen in Mexico City and got all sorts of valuable hands-on experience.)

3

DECIDE
&
DO

➡ Question. What would happen if you stopped being afraid of the word "no"?

I powered by the entrance to one of LA's top restaurants, Providence, trying not to get all sweaty-palmed from the fancy design. Trucking around the block, I had my sights set on the side entrance, for employees and deliveries. Several busboys talked in rapid-fire Spanish as they left work. I stopped the guys, clutching my résumé like a life vest.

"Hola! Está aquí el chef?" I said, asking for the chef in Spanish, smiling wide, to cover that I had no damn idea what I was doing. "I'd love to give him my résumé."

"Sí claro!" one guy said with a cheery smile, steering me into the restaurant's epic kitchen.

I breathed the heavenly scent of whatever was being prepped. Trying to identify the notes in the symphony of quiet but steady noises around me—loud gruff voices, hissing gas burners, sizzling oil, chopping knives. I'd suddenly stepped into a very serious, very professional, very no-nonsense kitchen, where the dozens of cooks were all moving with such urgency, and at such a fast clip, you'd think they were running to meet the president.

When I'd set out that morning, I'd felt pretty damn good. This was all part of my plan to take the taco world by storm, which I'd settled on as my new, post–Mexico City dream and plan. But, really, if I wanted to own any kind of a restaurant, I knew I should probably get hired by one first. Which had led me to get the nitty-gritty from a friend, who was a culinary vet. She had told me to go to restaurants between 2:00 and 4:00 p.m. Ask for the chef. Give him my résumé and tell him I wanted an opportunity to work in his kitchen. That made sense. So I'd gotten a list of ten of LA's best spots.

Which was how I'd ended up here.

But I wasn't a chef. I was a cook. I'd gone to restaurant management school, in Mexico, and the food words I knew were in Spanish. I had zero fucking idea how restaurants in the States worked. I didn't know what time they opened or closed. I didn't know what half the ingredients were. I was basically illiterate about everything related to the local culinary scene, except for how much I loved to cook, season, and eat food. *How did I let myself get talked into this?*

Well, I was desperate to act on my taco idea. I'd been back in LA for about six months, and I was already crying in my cereal, if you will. I was living with my mom again, at the ripe old age of twenty-four. I'd touched down right back where I'd left off, and yet, in the meantime, I had triumphed over a foreign country, managed my own house, made my own pesos, sold it all, and traveled the world. I'd come back a completely different, souped-up person—Ellen 2.0. But I was teetering on the edge of collapsing back into my old life. I had to get one of these restaurants to take a leap of faith on me, so I could launch my taco empire. The busboy at Providence had walked me back. Now, he stopped and pointed. "El chef está ahí," he said, indicating the chef.

And then he turned and disappeared into the dark hall behind him. *Oh my God*. The chef at Providence, Michael Cimarusti, is a big man with a BIG beard. He's got presence-and-a-half. He was standing there in the middle of his two Michelin star restaurant. (Thankfully, I didn't know much about these stars back then, or I would have really been shaking in my clogs.) I could immediately tell this place was legit. It felt like walking into the locker room of a professional sports team before a big game. Amid the pristine, wall-to-wall stainless steel, all the members of his kitchen staff were tricked out in matching uniforms, like an army, all moving with coordinated precision. Everybody present was clearly on a mission, so when someone without a mission walked in (i.e., me), it was very obvious. No one stopped working, even for a breath, but they definitely side-eyed the sudden show. What was happening was me, busting in, bright blue stretchy dress, big curls, part of my head shaved, with a ❤ cut into the side. Without breaking stride, everyone was clearly thinking: *Who IS this girl?* As I faced off against all of these serious, professional cooks, in this kitchen where everything had its proper place, I could already tell there was no room for anything that was less than perfect. To stay, I had to prove that there was a worthwhile reason for me to be allowed to take up space in this kitchen. And fast—everything around me was happening at double time. My Mexico City booth-babe muscle memory kicked in. Only, instead of selling them on canola oil or armored cars, now I was selling them on Ellen Bennett.

I walked right up to Chef, and at Mach speed, matching the urgency I felt around me (not a stretch—as anyone who knows me will attest, my resting speed is 80 mph).

"Hi, Chef, my name's Ellen Bennett," I said, careening right into my elevator pitch as to why he shouldn't kick my butt out of there. "I love your restaurant, love what you do, and would love the opportunity to work here. I just returned from living in Mexico for a while, and I am also Mexican and have the work ethic to prove it. Can I come and try out?" I said, ending on a high-pitched note, and with a gigantic smile. I may have practically been on my tippy toes.

By this point even the vegetables were watching, all with a look that said: *What the fuck is happening here?*

"OK, all right," Chef said, eyeballing the résumé I'd handed him, which, mind you, was a snooze-fest, and then, looking up to gauge my mettle, which, as I'd intuited, was what really mattered. "Why don't you come back the Friday after next, and we'll do a trial?"

YES! I thought. *I'm in!!!*

If the Front Door Isn't Open, Climb in Through the Window

→ If you're trying to sell someone on you or your dream, you can't half-ass it. You need to be fully present, fully awake, and fully certain of the direction you are steering your ship. Show up in person. Lead with humble enthusiasm. Slam dunk your pitch. The basic formula is:

☐ Ask someone you both know for an intro, and if you don't have an intro, go introduce yourself to whoever is in charge. Put yourself in a situation where you'll be near them. Send letters, DM them. Be resourceful on how to get ahold of people. Track them down somehow.

☐ Find a way to make you or your product known to them.

☐ Once you've gotten their attention, introduce yourself (be quick and humble).

☐ Describe why you love this company/person so much. (Be sincere—figure out what makes you love it, and be able to articulate that.)

☐ Make yourself useful. Think about what you can provide by the bushel that they don't already have, and offer it. Be helpful and solution-oriented, and you'll get your shots.

☐ Give a super-quick example, demonstrating your worth. Prove your value and land the opportunity, instead of demanding your worth and maybe not getting it.

☐ Give away some of your talents for free—which is not to say that you give your work away, but find a way to give people enough to believe in what you can deliver, and then they can give you the larger opportunity.

☐ Go above and beyond.

"What about this?" I replied, already negotiating. "I'll come in for the ENTIRE weekend, so you can really see how I work. I'll come Friday, Saturday, and Sunday. And then, you'll get a full picture. I think that'd be best."

"OK, yeah, sure," he said, already moving onto his next project, peering at it through his glasses.

"OK, great, thank you, Chef! I will see you next Friday."

"OK," he said, as everyone else gave me a look that was like: *Huh?* I walked out the same way I'd come in, cool as iceberg lettuce, but with a little more pep in my step. As soon as I was alone, outside the restaurant, I was beaming like a damn lighthouse. But if my time in Mexico City had left me with any magic beans of wisdom, it was to keep showing up, and not go home just because I'd aced an audition, no matter what. So I kept going. My next stop was another top restaurant. I burst in, résumé in hand, around 2:30 p.m. The owner/chef wasn't there, but her second-in-command was. I walked right up to him, emboldened by how well my last pit stop had gone.

"I'm looking for an opportunity to work here," I said, résumé outstretched in my hand, as I unleashed the same spiel that had worked so well at Providence.

"Oh, thanks, yeah, cool," he said. "We're not really hiring."

Around him, the kitchen staff chowed down family meal, watching me with these expressions of: *We're in the club. You're not.* Or at least that's how it felt to me.

"OK, well, thank you so much, and please let me know if you need stages, too—my info is on there," I said, working hard to keep the smile on my face until I got outside. He half smiled and then walked away. Well, so much for that! My inflated spirits let out a little of their air, as I realized Providence had probably been an anomaly, but . . . I had to keep going.

Of course, you can't stroll, uninvited, into nearly a dozen of the best restaurants in a food city like LA and get offered a shot in every one (or at least not with the résumé I had, and no personal referrals or references). No, I ate humble pie in the two days it took me to cross every restaurant off my list. But as I'd done with my auditions in Mexico City, I made it a point of pride to go to Every. Single. One. I just have to say, there is power in walking in and asking for an opportunity. Call it old-fashioned, or old-school; it's true that it doesn't happen nearly as much as it used to, so it makes an even bigger impact now. Try it on for size. Look someone right in the eye and ask them for an opportunity, and it just might work for you. Hand-written notes are in a similar boat—they really make an impression.

During my great restaurant résumé crawl, I also hit up Lazy Ox Canteen in LA's Little Tokyo neighborhood. And accidentally zipped right past the chef, Josef Centeno. When I got to the far end of the kitchen, I asked one of the dishwashers for intel.

"That's Chef over there," he said, nodding to Josef.

"OH," I said, scooting backward, red as a flaming pizza oven. "Hi, Chef," I said, giving him my résumé and my best sales pitch.

Unlike Chef Cimarusti at Providence, who was an intimidating figure in his sparkling white chef's coat, when I met Chef Josef he was wearing a T-shirt, jeans, a hat on backward, and boots that looked like they'd gotten some serious shit done. Chef Josef is so down-to-earth that I hadn't clocked that he was not only the chef, but also the kind of relentless dreamer, doer, and creator, who would soon open his own spots Bäco Mercat, Orsa & Winston, Bar Amá, and on and on. He also had the generosity of spirit to give me a listen.

"OK, yeah," he said, in his soft-spoken way, half-tilting his head toward me while I talked. "Why don't you come in on Thursday or Friday, and we'll try you out?"

"I'LL BE HERE! THANK YOU!"

I couldn't believe it.

Out of ten attempts, I'd landed two shots! Because I parked any shame in the trash can outside, showed up, and asked. And I didn't stop at no.

My dress rehearsal at Lazy Ox happened before Providence. On the next Friday night, drum roll please: I had my American restaurant kitchen debut. They threw me right into the fryer, too, or at least that was a part of my station in hot apps.

"I'm going to teach you a few dishes," the sous chef said, showing me the lay of the land. "We'll see how you do."

I am a notetaker. So in the midst of the full onslaught that is a busy kitchen line on a Friday night of service, I grabbed what was on hand—the blue painter's tape used to label things in the kitchen. I noted EVERY ingredient for every dish I learned on a different piece of tape, down to the garnish, including ones I couldn't have picked out of a lineup at the supermarket. "Sunchoke with espelette." I didn't know what a fucking sunchoke was, but I hurriedly scribbled down: Sunchoke (Whatever that knobby thing is). OK, good. But I really didn't know what an espelette was. (Note from 2021 Ellen, it's a French pepper.) And I knew even less about how to spell it, so I sounded it out and wrote: E-S-P-O-L-I-T.

I had no clue what I was doing, but I could move like a roadrunner and absorb like a sponge. So, I got to it, at my now completely recipe-tape-covered station. And my inborn need to keep moving in life was a perfect fit for a nonstop restaurant kitchen, where the to-do list is endless. An hour in, I'd learned the "pick up" for all of the dishes the sous chef had shown me. So, she showed me a few more dishes. And before I knew it, she walked away, and I was holding down one whole corner of that menu. Halfway through the night, I was working the entire station by myself. By closing time, I was offered a job at Lazy Ox.

Then, I went and tried out at Providence. I walked in, feeling shiny. Chef was nowhere to be seen. It was just his sous chef, Tristan, who everyone called T-Bone.

"Hi, I don't know if you guys remember me," I said. "Oh, I remember you all right," he said, with a big, T-Bone smirk.

He set me to my first task: A mountain of lemons. I was told to cut the skin, super thinly, and make diamond shapes, which meant needing a surgeon's knife skills. It literally took me three and a half hours. The entire kitchen turned TWICE, meaning we did prep to get ready for that night's service, cleaned, did family meal,

AND returned to the line. It was almost service, which is what the restaurant world calls the time when cooks are in service, making food, and being of service to customers. I was still cutting. Finally, Stephanie, the woman who needed the lemon zest triangles done, stopped by to grab them from me, saw my mangled attempts, shooed me aside and did the whole lot, perfectly, in twenty minutes. Ugh. I had already eaten dirt. And service was just starting. I wanted to crawl into the walk-in and hide myself away with my deli cup of shitty lemon cuts.

As service started, I stood by the plating area, just watching. First, I tried to leap up and help, but then I was batted back to the sidelines. It was like war, waged in these precise, synchronized movements, coordinated from one side of the kitchen to the other.

"Order in!" the expeditor would yell. "Five jon dory, pick up two lobsters, three uni."

Anyone related to that order would call it back to the expeditor, and then, before long, food would start to fly into the plating area. I swept and cleaned the floor, anytime nothing was being plated, just to stay helpful, but I always kept watching, asking cooks if I could help them with anything on their station. I was wheedling my way into the action. Little by little, I was allowed to run food to the plating area, put herbs on dishes, and dare I say, even run dishes to the dish pit. All I could think was: *Just keep moving.* By the end of the night, I had watched. I had asked questions. I had learned. Miraculously, I was still standing. The energy in the room felt like a freight train, and they'd allowed me to stand with them. All I could think was: *I want more.*

I was walking on air as I headed up to find T-Bone in his office upstairs.

"Soooooo, what do you think?" I asked. "Do I get the job? Can I work here?!"

He glanced over at me with a sheepish look.

"We aren't really hiring right now," he said.

Noooooooooo!!!! WTF? REALLY?!? Oh God. This is embarrassing . . . But wait. I already have my pinkie in the door. I can't just walk out now.

I had no idea what would come of any of this. I didn't have a crystal ball. But I was crystal clear that I was standing smack-dab in the middle of a Grade-A opportunity—to learn from amazing, talented, hardworking chefs who were doing the thing I knew I wanted to do. They were cooking incredible food with the most beautiful ingredients and making people happy. I absolutely needed to keep coming. Instead of focusing on what I could earn in the short-term, I zoomed back to look at the long-term picture. At what I wanted. And how I could maybe get it, if I gave a little. It seemed like this door was about to shut in my face. Well then, I'd just have to climb in through the window instead.

"Alright, well, I'd love to still keep coming, and learning, if you'll have me."

"OK, fine," he said, studying me like a shopping list. "You can do that."

He didn't have to tell me twice. I showed up for every shift with as much enthusiasm and grit as I could muster. I kept my eyeballs wide open. I asked a million questions, trying to soak up everything I could. I looked for openings to jump in and help. I cleaned like a lunatic. I learned every millimeter of that kitchen like it was my own. I never had even a single internal gripe about not receiving a paycheck. I was a stage (restaurant speak for an unpaid intern), being paid, and handsomely, in experience. And opportunity. And connection. For that, I was grateful. I let it beam out of me.

And after two weeks of this, Tristan came to me with the question: "How quickly can you quit your other job? We want to hire you."

And we were off to the races.

A note from future Ellen to my former self: A "no" can sometimes be a long-term "yes," if you don't immediately wave the white flag and give up. Keep going, always—even if it's just a millimeter forward, it's progress.

A lot of this has to do with perspective. I literally cannot even count on all of the fingers of all the chefs who wear my aprons how many doors have been slammed in my face along the way. Some might say that's the end of the story—they said "no." What about the other option? Think quick on your feet and find a way to stay present and be useful. Out of sight, out of mind is not helpful for landing a job, or a sale. Keep showing up. Make something that people need and value, and eventually, you will get a shot to work with them.

Another thing to keep in mind. If people say "no," that just means "no" right now, not forever. At least you're now in their

Understand the "No" So You Can Understand the "Why"

➤ Sometimes big ideas stall before leaving the station because we take "no" too literally. If we can understand the why behind the "no," we can often find a way to the other side. Turns out, just as often "no" means:

- ☐ "I'm in a bad mood."

- ☐ "Not yet."

- ☐ "I need more information."

- ☐ "I need time to think about it."

- ☐ "I'm not sure my boss will let me."

- ☐ "I'm feeling lazy."

- ☐ "The price isn't right."

- ☐ Or, my least favorite: "No, because this is how we've always done things."

What I Can Read Between the Lines:

"No, because I'm more comfortable with what I know, than I am investigating a new way of doing things, which scares/annoys/challenges/confuses/exhausts/overwhelms me."

What I Understand They Sometimes Really Mean :

"No, but if you can show me that your newfangled way won't be too uncomfortable or hard, and will actually be better, then, maybe, Yes."

◀

**With the
kitchen crew
at Providence,
circa 2013**

mental filing cabinet, and you're also maybe now a friend, which is what I value the most. People—boss, customer, or otherwise—are not transactions. They are all potential relationships.

See, when you look at it this way, that "no" from a minute ago— the one that felt like a jagged rejection, a steak knife through the heart—well, it probably didn't really have anything to do with you. And so, if you walked away in that moment, it's kind of on you. What if you'd stuck around, asked for more information, put some elbow grease into the potential for good feedback and a new friend, even if not necessarily a new customer? Maybe you'll be too nerved up and eager to get out of there the first few times you hear "no." I get it. Dealing with rejection is a skill that doesn't come naturally to most people. But that's why it's so important to practice doing this stuff in the real world. The more you do it, the easier it will get, and the more natural it will feel. And maybe once you hear "yes" a few times, you'll be encouraged enough to dig into the rejections, too.

When I walk into a situation, I show up as me. I look people in the eye. I give hugs. I ask a ton of questions. I get my hands into things, even before I'm invited to, sometimes. I am not shy about it, whether it's aprons or masks or whatever my new favorite topic is. Anyone who's ever met me will tell you this. I have found that this combination of being real and direct has been the foundation of getting other people to be as excited as I am.

Yes, this is partly just who I am. I understand that for the introverts out there, this might feel impossible. But I actually developed this side of my personality in a huge way in Mexico City when I had no safety net, and just had to keep putting myself out there, and trying, and making an impression, no matter how overwhelmed I sometimes felt. But even if that's not your experience, there are absolutely ways you can build yourself up. Take a public speaking class. Or an improv class (I did as a teenager). Get out of your comfort zone—it all helps!

Maybe their real-deal answer is a forever "no." But try to get some actual feedback (and that is equal in value to gold). Or see if you can come back later. Or have them send you down the street to their friend, who is looking for someone JUST LIKE YOU.

Any of those outcomes is a win, especially if you've made a new relationship. That's always a "yes."

4

Humble Enthusiasm

➡ **Remember how in 2012 I made Chef Josef forty aprons, pulled their ragged remains out of the fire, remade them, and emerged on the other end with zero dollars but a long-term customer?**

Not only that, but I'd also done my favorite thing—seen something I knew I could improve, and then actually made it come to life in the real world. What a freaking thrill. That right there was a new notch on my confidence belt.

After that, I was on a mission. I kept my day job—eek, my three day jobs—but I ate, slept, and breathed aprons.

I didn't have an office. I didn't have a website. I didn't have a copilot anymore—Kevin had abruptly announced that his heart wasn't in it and that I was better off on my own. I had a cell phone and I had Jose to do my sewing. I decided I would sell two types of aprons—full-size and "bistros," which were the kind that just go from the waist down. There was a notebook that I planned to write my orders in, and I had a Mini Cooper, which was stuffed to the gills with fabric samples and rolled up finished aprons.

◄

Moving H&B headquarters from my house to our first actual office in 2013

Well, it turned out having a great idea and one happy customer wasn't enough to kickstart an entire company. I definitely had a leg up because I worked at two legit restaurants that everyone in the LA food scene knew and respected. That gave me credibility. But success was still a long shot. I was trying to sell something that had never been looked at this way before. Because most restaurants rented their linen, including aprons, they were sort of an afterthought. And sure, the fabrics were kind of shabby and ugly, but they were soooo cheap and only for the back-of-the-house cooks. And so what? They had always been OK. Out of nowhere, I was making a premium apron that would cost four or five times what they were used to paying. I knew there was a risk of hearing: "Are you out of your mind? This is insane."

But I knew there was a better way. The deeper why of H&B was immediately obvious when people put on one of our aprons. The gear you wore made you look and feel the part, and therefore made you want to crush it in the kitchen, no matter if you were the chef, or a commis (a chef-in-training), or a line cook. Even if the aprons seemed expensive upfront, compared to rental costs, they were an investment. Your team would be wearing gear that was higher quality, looked awesome, lasted longer, and, in some cases, was customized to match your branding. It had always been as important as the knife they used in their kitchen, and now just as much care would go into making it.

Plus, if we cared enough to put in the blood, sweat, and knife skills required to prepare some of the best food in the country, why

H&B Apron Design

➤ **With these improvements, our design drop-kicked the usual cheap, poly-cotton aprons**

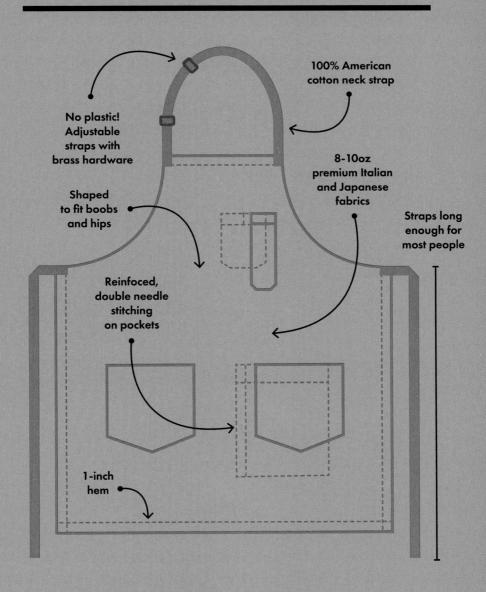

No plastic! Adjustable straps with brass hardware

100% American cotton neck strap

Shaped to fit boobs and hips

8-10oz premium Italian and Japanese fabrics

Straps long enough for most people

Reinfoced, double needle stitching on pockets

1-inch hem

couldn't we have gear with that same level of quality and properness? Why shouldn't we have brass hardware, Japanese denim, or that special stitching on the chest? Instinctively, I knew I had hit on a good idea at the right moment. Now I had to build it, from the ground up.

This is an awkward but crucial stage! Your dream won't truly have legs until you can bring other people on board for the adventure. That's what gives the idea legitimacy and permanence. It's true if you're launching a new company, a new side hustle, or a grand plan of any kind. You have an idea for something people actually need or want; they just haven't realized it yet. People aren't mind readers, so it's your job to let them know what you're offering, what problem your product is solving, and educate them on why they need it, with excitement and conviction.

This crew is going to be your home base on your journey. If you keep them happy, they're going to be your best source of early feedback and your most ardent evangelists, helping spread the word about the magic you are making. Every tribe looks different. And my apron squad was also unique to me and my product. Getting my first customers for my fledgling business entailed finding the people who would believe in my vision, who would get the importance of my deeper why: being proud of the gear you wear.

On most days, I had to run to Providence, or Bäco, to clock in by 3:00 p.m. On my "lunch break," at 4:00, I would hop out to the parking lot, with my family meal on a melamine plate, deli cup in hand, and take conference calls in my car.

"Super excited to hear about what you guys are up to and looking for," I would begin warmly (because I was genuinely excited—don't be fake, people can smell BS a mile away). "Has your team ever worn an H&B apron? Because we're using insane materials, they'll last four to five times longer (true story). Your staff is going to love their uniforms because they're super comfortable and they fit better, and we can also brand them for your restaurant."

But I always had to keep one eye on the time, and grind things to a halt as seamlessly as possible when my mealtime was up.

"Well, guys, that was super helpful, thanks for sharing everything, I'm so glad we're working together," I said, in conclusion. "My team is excited that we are collaborating on this. We'll be in contact soon. Thank you so much!"

Little did they know, a minute later, I was bolting back inside, tying on my own apron, and sliding back into my station to get those damn oysters shucked.

I always led my pitches with the "why" of H&B, because I knew that I had figured out a better way. And if I could only get in front of enough chefs and restaurant owners to explain it to them, they'd soon be converts. It wasn't just what I was there to tell them—it was *how* I was telling them: with a boatload of humble enthusiasm. I listened more than I talked, but I always kept the volume cranked up to eleven—chefs work twelve-hour shifts, on a short day, and if they were giving me their time, I was damn well going to make good use of it.

It was from watching and listening closely that I realized that,

HUMBLE ENTHUSIASM
=
EXCITED TO SHARE

What
you know

+

EXCITED TO LEARN

What
you don't
know

always, asking for advice was a better sales strategy than, you know, selling.

One Sunday, I was headed over to the Santa Monica Farmers' Market, the favorite stomping ground of lots of the city's major chefs, carrying the few apron samples I had at the time. Lo and behold, I caught sight of one of my bosses, Donato Poto—the very Italian, smiley co-owner and front-of-the-house capo honcho at Providence. He came over to scope out my modest display: a few colorful aprons draped across a foldable table, a homemade sign, and some DIY business cards. I'd paid twenty dollars for a rubber stamp of the H&B logo. And I'd gone to Staples and picked up some precut business cards in the heaviest card stock they carried.

As we were talking, I noticed another familiar face topped with spiky dark hair. *Is that. . . . ?*

"That's Chef Josiah Citrin!" I said. "He has two Michelin stars!"

"Come here," Donato said, laughing, always full of good cheer, and ready to help. He walked me over to Josiah and introduced me with his usual flair.

"This girl works at Providence," Donato said in his thick but friendly Italian accent, with a giant smile on his face. "She is also selling aprons."

There are few stamps of quality in the LA restaurant scene that are higher karat gold than Donato's, so Josiah stopped and gave me his attention.

"Um, hi! Yes, I work at Providence, and it's true I'm making

How to Sell Without Making People Feel Like a Transaction

◼ Give a brief overview of why you're doing what you do.

◼ Flip the script and make it about them. Ask questions about their place, space, what they're doing. And find things you love about their project. Everyone has a story, and you want to understand theirs, because, after all, you are there to genuinely help them.

◼ Ask questions about what they hope for and need, what they want, in order to figure out what you can do to help them get there.

◼ Listen like you're a freakin' doctor, and you are trying to diagnose your patient's ailments—what is working, what isn't working, what hurts, what's broken, what makes them happy. LISTEN. (Lots of people can ask questions but forget to actually listen to the answers.) LISTEN TO THEM FOR REAL.

■ Take notes, emphatically, so you don't forget anything.

■ Ask follow-up questions to get to the deeper reasons behind their first responses.

■ Be sure to understand what they want. Then, you can either show them physically what you can do, and brainstorm and collaborate there together, or send a follow-up proposal. Either way, repeat back what you got from them. For me, this was something like: "OK, yep, I'm loving this, so you're hoping for something fun and clean with a little pop of color, and let's stick to a color or two, max."

■ Be human and relatable—don't be a robot!

■ Be efficient with your time and theirs. Keep it short and sweet. Get the info you need, hit on the points you want to make, show them what you need to show them, and then get your buns out of there.

■ Use your emotional intelligence to gauge interest levels and if they seem busy, stressed, or now need to do something else.

■ Be proactive and recap what YOU are going to do as next steps and mention if they should do anything, too, and then let yourself out.

---

aprons now," I said, warming up to a full boil and delivering the forty-second version of my pitch with as much gusto as possible.

Josiah didn't give me a definite yes, but he did invite me to come visit him at his mother ship of dining excellence, Mélisse. (I felt like leaping out of my apron, but I played it cool, obviously.) When I showed up at his office with samples, I decided to ask him for his thoughts and make it more about his input than my aprons.

"I brought a bunch of different colors, and I want to get your input," I said. "We're working in all different styles and we haven't quite landed on which cuts and what versions we're going to lead with. I would love your thoughts, to learn what you need, to hear what you think, and if there's anything I can change, and fix, and improve. We are working at it to make it better."

By doing this, I was getting his input and buy-in. There was no mention of trying to sell him an apron. There was simply a passion for showing him what I had to offer—inviting him to hold the fabric, asking him what he thought, and if he could offer me any feedback that could help me to make it better. I took his feedback to heart, and what started out as a helpful-advice visit turned into Josiah placing an order. I internally celebrated for a split second, and then I was all about getting back to work and making this happen. For the first few years of H&B, I was always waiting for the other shoe to drop, so I kept thinking: *If I just run fast enough, maybe I can keep this all from grinding to a stop.*

In my first six months, H&B became a giant, powerful magnet. It pulled in my first helpers, who were friends, and friends of

> **Be gracious.** <mark>Even a "no" is valuable when it comes with information</mark> that could help you to improve, or leaves the door open for a future relationship.

friends, who took up the H&B cause and offered to give me a hand in their spare time. (HUGE shout out to my first employees, Marissa and Allie.) Our passion for what we were doing was as much of a calling card as my aprons were. And it only grew from there. The first chefs were like seeds that got swept up by a great gust of wind and spread into a whole field of new H&B fans.

As the one-year anniversary of H&B approached, I was googly-eyed at the fact that we had begun to have a following. I had customers and people who also cared, just like I did! At the outset of H&B, the quest was a chef-by-chef, street-by-street adventure to share Hedley & Bennett with as many people as possible. A big part of my weekly outreach was emailing or texting after I met a chef at an event, or after I'd been referred by another chef. Like when I'd met Chef Jonathan Benno down at the Strand House in Manhattan Beach and wiggled my way into a face-to-face meeting back at his restaurant in New York City, via one humbly enthusiastic email.

Date: Thu, Oct 3, 2013 at 8:39 PM
Subject: Hedley&Bennett Apron Girl:)

Hi Jonathan!

It was really nice meeting you recently. :)
I am reaching out to you because I am actually planning on
going to NYC next week and would love to come see and
visit your kitchen!

I also wanted to ask you if you have any chefs or restaurants
that you think I should reach out to.

I really want to bring Hedley&Bennett to New York but it is
slightly newer territory to us so I could use a little guidance,
there's just SOOO many restaurants!

I appreciate the help so much!
Hope to see you next week!

Talk soon,
Ellen, the apron lady:)

CHEF MADE GOOD ON HIS WORD and invited me to stop by
Lincoln. I rolled up around 3:00 p.m., in between lunch and dinner
service. Walking in off the street and into the front of the restaurant was like going underwater into an alternate world. I stepped

An Interview with Chef Benno

➡ After our meeting at the Strand House in Manhattan Beach, Chef Jonathan Benno agreed to let me stop by his restaurant at the time, Lincoln. Plus, he was generous enough to email-introduce me around New York City, where I was trying to break in at the time. Here's how he remembers it:

"When she came to New York, I was working at Lincoln Restaurant on the Upper West Side . . . and I was able to make a couple of introductions for her. I know that she was obviously well established and well loved in Los Angeles, and she took all of that goodwill and she brought it to New York and made friends, obviously, very quickly. She still is very, very generous with not just her time, but her aprons, and now her gear—the product line has grown.

". . . I always see her, and it's fun and, like, 'Hey, look at this new apron I'm working on.' But she was able to really break into a very difficult niche, if that's the right word, in chef gear. That market is kind of oversaturated. There's just a lot of noise, and a lot of people competing for attention. But she's really got a quality product. It's not cheap in the market. It's definitely on the expensive side, but like most things in life, you get what you pay for. You're paying for labor, and you're paying for quality of ingredients, like the quality of material. [The aprons] are really, really, really well-made, very durable . . . She has a cook's perspective and of course knows, and hangs out, and talks to a gazillion people across the industry. So, she has one foot in the garment business and one foot in the hospitality industry. I don't know the business side of Ellen, but what I do know is her personality, and her spirit, and her drive."

What made you take time in your day that you didn't really have to send those emails, introducing Ellen around New York City?

"I still don't feel like I did a lot, but, you know, people helped me along the way. So, I mean, you're right, I don't have a lot of time, but people helped me, so if I have an opportunity—and what did it really take for me to send a couple of emails and make a couple of phone calls? You know, twenty minutes, oh my god, thirty minutes? But look what I got out of it. I mean, I made this incredible friend. So that was definitely time well spent. And it was one hundred percent her spirit. I'm not going to go out of my way for someone if I don't truly believe in that person. And Ellen, her spirit is really—you can almost feel it in the room—it's electric. And of course, the product is high quality. It's made in Los Angeles. So, I just bought into the whole thing from the beginning. I was skeptical about the business model in such a competitive market. But, hey, every once in a while, it's nice to be wrong. She did it."

What was that first kitchen visit to Lincoln like?
"When they make the movie [about Ellen's life], that [visit] will be in there. Again, she's so generous that she doesn't go back to Los Angeles with those bags of aprons. Those are samples, and gifts for people, and maybe a small order for John, or oh gosh, French Bistro needs more of these aprons, I'll come up—I'm gonna bring them to them. So yeah, and me being from the East Coast, she stands out a little bit, like: 'Lady, you are not from here,' with the bright clothing, and literally talking to every person on the street. And two giant canvas bags of aprons and gear. She is a force, that's for sure."

Being a chef requires passion and attention to detail— did you see a kindred spirit?
"One hundred percent, and again, she worked in the kitchen. I know she worked at Providence. That's a grown-up restaurant. That's a serious place, that's a serious kitchen. Michael and his team—talk about being meticulous, and sourcing great ingredients, and attention to detail. I'm not saying she got all that from Providence and Michael and his team, but boy, it sure helps to spend time in that environment. I mean that's a remarkable place, and he's a remarkable human being."

into the calm, pristine dining room where men in suits painstak-
ingly polished wine glasses. Then the world transformed again, as
I passed through a doorway into the brightly lit kitchen, and the
loud, hot, chaotic military campaign on the other side. I was lugging a giant cube of aprons in a big bag, but I knew how to maneuver
my way through the sounds of clanging pot lids, whirring dishwashers, and gurgling oil, with cooks yelling, "Behind," to warn others of
their location in the cramped space, as they whizzed through with
hot pans and time-sensitive concoctions.

"Welcome to Lincoln," Chef said.

"Thank you! I'm so excited to be here!"

Chef showed me around, with my big bag of aprons hanging off
my shoulder and whipping around behind me, trying to stay out of
the way while sticking my nose into everything. I wasn't thinking
about the pitch I was about to give, or about the sale that might happen. I was right there in the moment, learning what made Lincoln
so special.

"Hi! Hi! That looks delicious. Hi!" I said to everyone we passed.

"Ooh, this looks so good, can I try?" I said, gathering goodies
and munching as I went.

When we were heading back to Chef's office, we passed the
pastry chef.

"Do you want one?" she said, smiling, and nodding toward rows
of beautiful macarons.

"Of course I want one! Thanks!!"

I popped the macaron into my mouth, and it dissolved with

sweet good perfection. As we walked by the giant walk-in refrigerator, I was struck by the sign that hung there:

"If you don't have time to do it right, when will you have time to do it over?"

Oh wow, that's so true! I thought, mentally filing away for later both the quote itself and the practice of lining your workspace with bursts of inspiration.

His office was so small and narrow that the computer screen was mounted on the wall, because there was really nowhere else for it to go. But he had the H&B apron I'd given him during our first meeting, hung up as well. I'd seen his world; now it was time to show him mine.

I thumped the bag of aprons down on his chair and started pulling them out.

"OK, let's see what we've got," I said. "I've got a bunch of stuff you can look at."

"Great," he said, leaning in to see what was on offer. "Before you get too big in New York, I want to make sure I've got some aprons for myself."

While we were talking, I was putting him in an apron, and pointing out all of the features, like the adjustable neck strap on top, and spinning him around and tugging on the apron and getting it to fall just so, and tying up the back.

"We reinforce every pocket, reinforce all the corners, so it's super durable," I said. "We made sure it has a chest pocket. Do you like the placement? Oh, and we added a loop, not on all of the aprons, but on some of them. This is one of my favorite fabrics. It's so soft and breathable and it just feels really nice."

He seemed to be having just as much fun as I was. He was answering my questions and putting his hands on the fabric, and trying out the pockets, and just getting a good feel for it. But I wasn't done yet. I put him into each of the aprons I had brought, showing him the subtle but important differences between the fabrics, and letting him have options. Finally, out of all of the styles and fabrics, he found one that he loved.

"Awesome, let's do five of those," he said, indicating his favorite. "This one is great."

So, yes, I'd made a sale. And I was pleased as fruit punch that we were going to be outfitting the chefs at Lincoln. But that wasn't the most important thing that happened that day. Because I'd come in with my antennae up and my genuine curiosity and desire to connect ablaze, Chef imparted a great honor on me. He showed me an apron he'd been given by his mentor, the great Thomas Keller, who he'd come up under at French Laundry in California, and then Per Se in New York City, working for him for twenty years. When he'd left to run his own kitchen, Thomas Keller gave him one of two commis aprons he'd had made by Hermes, in the signature shade that has become known as Thomas Keller blue. There were only two of them in the whole world. One had been auctioned off at a charity event, and he had the other one, and he was putting it into my hands. The apron represented this idea, championed by Chef Keller, and now by Chef Benno, of working hard, and never not learning.

"One day when I have my own restaurant, I'm going to hang it up there," he said. "I want you to have this until then. When I do, you can give it back to me. But until then, I want you to hold onto this. I think it's in better hands with you than it was with me. Just hold onto it."

"Of course, Chef, thank you so much," I said.

Here was this person, who was like a leader, and a thought partner, and just such a respected bastion of excellence in the restaurant world—literally a Godfather-type person—and he was handing me this apron that he'd gotten from his mentor. It felt like a knight entrusting me with his sword. I was so moved and gobsmacked.

We wrapped the apron in plastic so it wouldn't get damaged or stained, and when I got back to LA, I hung it behind my desk, moving it from office to office, until six years later, Chef Benno did in fact open his own restaurant, and I was so thrilled to send it back to him. Until then, when I looked at that apron, I always thought about how this very sentimental object represented collaborative growth, humble enthusiasm, and a constant craving to learn more and get better, all the foundations on which I wanted to build and grow H&B.

In the meantime, the apron lady had made a new friend, and H&B had earned a passionate champion. I cannot even count all of the people that Chef Benno brought me to, and not just when we happened to be at a food festival together, and it was easy to turn around and make a quick intro. I'm talking about so, so many emails that he personally took the time out of his overpacked schedule to send on my behalf—to other chefs, Eli Kaimeh at Per Se, Gavin Kaysen at Daniel, David Chang at Momofuku—to the editors of *Food & Wine*, where I met Dana Cowin, who became a great and lasting mentor. And because Chef was so respected, I always got an audience thanks to his note on my behalf, and I usually got a new squad member.

No matter how many new squad members we added, I looked at each and every one as a copilot, moving us toward a shared goal— the perfect apron! I couldn't believe it! I was building a community, and now the community was starting to expand on its own. I didn't have to fight for every next order. Hedley & Bennett was becoming known for something.

A year and a half in, we had more than a hundred styles and sizes and colors and choices. And it only snowballed from there. Martha Stewart, Jacques Pepin. The fine folks at Shake Shack, Facebook, SpaceX. Chef Ludo from Petit Trois. The women's chef coat. The men's chef coat. Leather aprons. Gardeners' aprons. Barbers' aprons. Aprons. Aprons. Aprons. It was all a beautiful goddamn blur of denim, and brushed canvas, and pockets, pockets, everywhere. By 2014, we were making thousands of aprons a week.

● ● ●

TO BUILD YOUR SQUAD, you have to meet your people where they are. If they're within reach of your network, like mine were, make as much beautiful noise as you can to attract their time, energy, and attention. If your people are elsewhere, find a way to intersect your path with theirs. Give your squad every opportunity to find you. Don't hide, even unintentionally, in plain sight.

When squad-building, you aren't trying to win over everyone, just the stakeholders who are aligned with your mission and your way of thinking. Those are your people.

The fear of sharing your idea is real, but getting buy-in from other people will elevate how you see your business and your product. This makes your idea, concept, product, whatever it may be, bigger than you. It becomes about all these other people, too, and the mission that you are trying to spread. When things get sticky, hairy, or downright miserable, you will rely on this squad, this mission, this feeling, to get you through those dark points, I promise.

◄

**Some of
our original
H&B squad,
circa 2014**

SPECIAL SECTION

Listen, Really Listen

→ I WAS TRIPPING ON SUNSHINE the whole way over to meet Chef Vinny at Animal, one of the top restaurants in LA.

I burst into the kitchen, as usual, this time hopped up to hand him his five, super-custom black aprons in beautiful Italian chambray.

Vinny seemed genuinely excited to try his apron on. He slid it over his head, made it over his scraggly beard, and set about cinching up the belt. Tugged at the tie. Yanked at the straps. There was no getting around it: the apron didn't quite fit. The straps tied in the back, but the fabric looked tight and uncomfortable.

"I'm a hefty guy," Vinny said good-naturedly. "I kind of want to be able to fit more in over time, just in case, you know, for room to grow."

Adrenaline rushed through my whole body. It felt a little bit like somebody had just squeezed my stomach, whoosh, and all of the air was suddenly gone.

Oh my god, did that just happen? I promised an apron that would make him feel great in his skin and I did . . . the opposite? Yep, that happened. Alright. OK. There's a solution to this. Just listen!

This was not at all the outcome I'd been hoping for, but instead of making excuses about how it was right, or trying to talk my way out of it, I leaned into his feedback.

"Tell me more," I said.

"I love the apron," he said. "I love the style. But I want something that I can be wrapped into, that's much bigger than this."

Fuck.

"OK, yeah, I know what you're saying!" I said. "What were you thinking? Let's see what we can do."

"I want . . . room-to-grow waist straps," he said with a chuckle.

"Room-to-grow straps, yes!" I said.

As we were talking, I was chewing and tasting and swallowing and digesting his feedback. I immediately knew this would raise the cost of the apron, because each strap would require more webbing. But it was just the kind of attention-to-detail touch that would make our aprons stand out. More people would be able to fit into them, and that would mean more potential happy squad members.

Now, rewind back to my first order for Chef Josef and remember that I'd already devoted serious brain hours to working and reworking those damn neck straps. And I'd been pretty sure they were damn near perfect. Except not the waist straps. Was I thrilled to have to work on the straps again? Not exactly. But I saw a way to improve my product, and I knew I had to take it.

It seemed like every week there was a new wall to climb. After the straps, then it was the hardware. And then, the pockets were too small. And then, they were attached incorrectly. And mind you, this wasn't just information I was getting from some anonymous online survey. These were real chefs I liked and respected, looking me in the eye and telling me what the fuck was wrong with my aprons. While big companies hire consulting firms to identify the opportunities in their new market, I got out there and asked a million questions to anyone who would take a meeting with me. To this day, the Animal aprons are among the products that I'm most proud of, and the room-to-grow-strap has become *the* strap.

It's so tempting to settle at "good enough." I get it. But think about it this way. Most people give up when it starts to get hard. If you are one of the few who keeps going, and who takes the setbacks you face as fuel to go further and do better, your chances of success are that much higher. The main reason I push myself is that I know, if I'm having a hard time and I want to knock off, as enticing as that may seem, if I just keep going a little longer, all my efforts might pay off. But if I give up now, I didn't ever get to the finish line. It's like forfeiting the marathon at mile seventeen. Sure, it might feel better in the moment, but what happened to the seventeen miles you just killed yourself on—what's the payoff in stopping short? There is none.

By not overlooking the little things I could do to improve my aprons, I took them from good, to better, to actually amazing—and we're still reworking them to this day.

But, here comes *the big but*, I plunged first, then tweaked. Dream first, details later. Restaurants seemed to appreciate my hands-on, collaborative approach. I was helping to tap into the lightbulb of aprons as a tool, all from the line cook's perspective. Plus, in Vinny's case, he was just as happy to give me feedback as I was to hear it. Sometimes, though, you might have to encourage people by having some questions at the ready.

NOT Taking Feedback Is NOT an Option

→ You should always be seeking feedback and using it to improve. In order to get game-changing intel, you have to draw it in. Here are some of the tricks that have always worked for me:

☐ Sit down face-to-face, especially if the conversation is difficult. Or at least call.

☐ Park any defensiveness at the door and really be willing to listen.

☐ Don't rush. Acknowledge and take the time to understand each point as it's made.

☐ If there's a reason to apologize, because something didn't live up to its promise, do so.

☐ Dig deeper. Ask follow-up questions. Ask for the other person's why.

☐ Sometimes it's necessary to explain why their idea won't work/could be stronger.

☐ Be as fully present as possible. This means sleeping enough, eating enough, getting exercise. Starting a new venture is running a marathon and the body and mind need fuel.

6 Questions to Ask to Go from Good to Awesome

(1) What's working?

(2) What's not working?

(3) If there's an issue with the product or service you received, what would you consider a successful resolution?

(4) If you're on the fence about our relationship, what would be a deal breaker for you?

(5) If there is an issue, what if we can't resolve it specifically? Is there another way we could make it up to you?

(6) What else do you wish we had thought of?

5

KEEP GOING, KEEP CREATING

➡ During the first few years of H&B, we were a lean operation and we all wore multiple hats.

But I spent a lot of time begging what team I did have—my sewers, salespeople, and sometimes–production managers—to work faster, make fewer mistakes, and put out fires. Well, I alternated between pleading and yelling.

Here are just a few of the doozies from the lore of early H&B:

☐ The time we were so tight on a deadline for getting an apron to Jamie Oliver for a charity event he was hosting, I literally flew someone to London to hand-deliver it (not particularly cost effective).

☐ Another time, we missed the shipping cutoff for getting some aprons to the Food & Wine Classic in

Aspen, and had two employees drive them there (a fourteen-hour trip).

- ☐ The great Pantone disaster, when we accidentally used the wrong shade of chartreuse thread for the custom embroidery on the aprons for Top Chef Richard Blais. But we didn't realize it until the aprons were already sewn, shipped, and received with frustration and disappointment by Chef (understandably).

These might not sound that bad when you read them like this, but in the moment, as a small business, they were monstrous blows to our confidence and to our bank account.

I was still years away from seeing my own role in the dysfunction junction that was the production pipeline at H&B. I didn't have an MBA. I had no fashion background. And I was too fucking busy. The result was that we had no official production processes in place. There was no real system—not at any stage of the production chain, from us tossing the orders at the sewers, to them handing the aprons back (often with mistakes), to us finally getting the orders out to our customers (often late). As long as we got orders out—even if it was just barely—I focused on the relief and success at the end of the day, not the six dozen heart attacks that had occurred during the previous twenty-four hours.

One of our biggest heart attacks happened in January 2013.

December 2012, One Month Before the Volt Deadline

It all started when I was cooking up a food storm with my Providence crew for a special event at Michael Voltaggio's restaurant, Ink. His brother, Bryan, slipped a piece of paper into my pocket. I opened it and read: I need 100 aprons.

Holy shit. That would be one of our biggest orders, ever. Not only that, but the aprons would be for the opening of Bryan's huge new DC-area spot, Volt, which was launching in a matter of weeks. Yikes! But there was no way I was going to say no to a massive order for a major player in the food world, so I dug in and set out to get it done.

I didn't hesitate to check my inventory, consult my sewers, or ask myself if this was even possible. Of course, future Ellen is shaking her head at young Ellen, thinking: Oh boy. But when you're starting out, you don't know what you don't know.

We were going to will this into existence, even if it killed us!

So I just put a big X on the calendar, like *this is the day that the order needs to be out, period.* Note that there was no scheduled check-in along the way to make sure we were on track for our delivery date. I never stopped and reckoned: Well, if it takes one sewer so many hours to make one apron, and I need 100 aprons in twenty-one days, then . . .

In my magical realism mindscape, the only possible vision was of a successful outcome.

And then, the madness.

4 Things That Were Happening in My Company (Some of Which I Didn't Know Were Happening)

(1) **Mistakes were the norm**, like aprons with the wrong colors and incorrect embroidery. People were untrained and not managed correctly, so when these mistakes happened, they weren't being shared.

---

(2) Customers' **complaints were often falling between the cracks** until they were totally irate.

---

(3) **Deadlines were missed**, leading to expensive overnight shipping bills ($200-$500) for big orders.

---

(4) Different departments were **pointing fingers** at each other for any and all errors.

"How are those aprons coming along?" I asked. "We getting close?"

"Oh, I'm sorry, Ellen, but my brother got stabbed yesterday," my sewer said. "I had to go to the hospital. I will finish this week. I promise."

Um, what?!

"What?! Is he OK? Are you OK?! What do you mean, he got stabbed? OMG. I really needed these done. What am I going to do? The order has to go out FRIDAY."

"Yes, yes, you will have them."

They had said that YESTERDAY, but OK. I had three meetings all over town, and two other orders that needed to go out, and a million other details to nail down, plus I was due over at Providence by 3:00 p.m. for my usual line cook shift. (One year into Hedley & Bennett, and with three employees at the office, I was still holding onto my line cook job at Providence.) So I scampered back to our office to get on with it. This kept up until the morning of our shipping deadline. I ran down the flight of stairs to where our sewers were. The order still wasn't ready.

My already palpable panic spiked higher as I entered the chaos of their workspace—a tsunami of fabric exploded from literally every available space in the tiny room—my aprons, items for other clients; cheap imported clothes they were selling wholesale. It was enough to give you an asthma attack. A bag of half-eaten Cheetos slumped on top of an in-progress apron, the biohazard orange cheese dust millimeters away from spilling out and adding its own surreal accent. Takeout containers and other snacks and half-drunk cans of soda were scattered around everywhere.

I implored, and pushed, and said with audible pain and fear: "We can't be late!" I yelled. Beaming every ounce of energy and need for these aprons to be done squarely at our sewers. It wasn't fun, for me or for them, but it had worked before. Not this time, though. The aprons were simply not done yet. But that was OK, because we could still overnight them via FedEx the next day.

Since every single order was custom in those days, it was easy for errors to sneak in. Often, there were 911-style emergencies, because we'd run out of fabric, or D-rings, or some other essential item. We didn't have a regular supplier for anything, which meant I scared up our supplies from a variety of retail fabric stores and suppliers as best as I could, often while in SOS mode.

• • •

WHEN THE NEXT DAY DAWNED, they still weren't done, and now, the opening was TOMORROW night. But, well, as long as we had them by the end of the day, we could overnight them, no matter the cost. I practically counted every stitch coming out of the sewers' machines on that long, agonizing afternoon, but nope, the sewers didn't meet our deadline. By the time we finally got our hot little paws on the stack of aprons, it was too late to drop them off at our local FedEx spot. Which led to me, apron-crazed, frantic, panicked Ellen, speeding down the highway to LAX with my top salesperson

The Nitty-Gritty

➤ After the first full year, when I quit my full-time job at Providence, we were selling aprons from $38 for a bistro to $85 for a full apron, retail, and offering industry discounts for anyone in the restaurant/hotel/coffee/hospitality world. Without realizing it, we were simultaneously building a D2C and a B2B business. Each channel had different pricing. And our numbers were roughly:

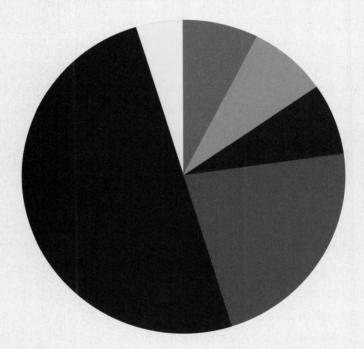

■ **Cost of Making Aprons** (Material, Production)

Sales (Travel, Advertising, Subscriptions)

■ **Payroll**

■ Profit

Manufacturing (Rent, Transportation, Supplies, Maintenence)

■ **Corporate** (Bank fees, Insurance, Office, Legal, Accounting)

and chief copilot, Marissa in the passenger seat. We would have driven right up onto the tarmac and hand-carried those aprons onto the FedEx plane—that's actually what we were intending to do. Of course, in reality, a chain-link fence topped with barbed wire stopped us.

"Can I help you?" the security guard outside the LAX tarmac asked us.

"Yes, sir! We're trying to get to the FedEx airplane dock."

Needless to say, the security guard was only too happy to disillusion us about whether we would be allowed to pull my Mini Cooper up to the FedEx airplane dock. Instead, we could drop off our package at a FedEx location like any normal, *sane* person.

The aprons were not going to make it. It was a harpoon of hurt and a big wake-up call. All those other times we'd missed a deadline, we'd Scooby-Dooed some crazy work-around and saved the day. But not today. There was no driving the aprons to DC overnight. We'd failed.

I stood outside the chain-link fence, dumbfounded. Crushed.

My hustle and determination had always been enough, and for the first time, standing in the dark with a hatchback full of aprons, I came up short.

I had truly, without a doubt, undeniably, failed. And it stung like a bitch. I'd always kind of thought the world would just love me, and I would love the world, and everything would be peachy and roses, until the end of time. Nope, not that day. As we all know, losing your innocence hurts through and through. But I didn't have any time to stop and triage my own battle wounds. Tomorrow was on the verge of dawning, with its next bushel of orders that absolutely had to go out IMMEDIATELY. Plus, I had emails to answer about in-process orders, and chefs to call back about the seedlings of eventual orders. Peppering everything else was the ping of texts from my helpers who had questions and updates for me, which needed my attention. But I had to deal with the mess in my lap.

Thankfully, I had the good sense to tune out all of the noise and to pay attention to the million-watt lightbulb that losing my business innocence had caused to suddenly turn on over my head: *starting a business is not for the faint of heart.* Up until then, yes, there'd been late nights and stressful last-minute bailouts, but mostly everything had been coming up daisies, in terms of how welcoming chefs had been, and how inspiring the design process was, and how glowing the press I'd started receiving was—fun pieces in *Fast Company*, the *LA Times*, *Food & Wine*, about this cute little line cook with a new kind of apron company. I'd thought that was having a business. But that was just the glaze on the cinnamon bun, which really was this: to own a business means to own the mistakes.

With my tail between my legs, I called Bryan's assistant to relay the bad news. There was no one else to do it, and even if there had been, I would have made the call myself. It's never more important to show up for someone than when you have to let them down. I was going to take my lumps and see what I could do to make it right. My palms clammed up and my heart raced. I took long, deep breaths as I called her.

"Hi there, how are you?" I said softly. "I wanted to let you know what happened. Unfortunately, we weren't able to make the cut off. We are so sorry. The aprons are ready, but they didn't make it onto the plane. We tried to get them there. We really did, but unfortunately, we missed the pickup window. We did everything we could, but we just didn't get them there. We're going to overnight them tomorrow. And again, I'm so sorry about this."

There was a long silence on the phone. I could tell that she was taking in the fact that she was now going to have to go and tell all of this to her boss.

"I'm really sorry," I said again.

"Thanks for letting me know," she said. "I'll talk to Chef. This is disappointing, to say the least. I know not everything is in your control, but we had talked about this date."

She wasn't responding with raging anger, but I felt it all the same.

We ended up not charging them anything for the order—nada for the money it would cost to overnight a hundred aprons across the country (of course) and zilch for the aprons themselves. Yes, the fine folks at Volt survived. And, yes, we survived (even if our monthly budget didn't). But that right there was a serious hockey stick to the face.

This was the beginning of a slow realization—one that took years to sink in, I'm embarrassed to say—that processes exist to allow for and to support creativity, not to disrupt it. Eventually, you have to step out of survival mode in order to thrive. It's the brutal truth of being a founder. Yes, leap. Yes, run. Yes, get up when you get knocked down and try again. Yes, do all of these things on repeat, most likely for years, even when it seems impossible, and seems like you should finally throw in the towel because it's just too hard. . . . Well, you take a deep breath, pick up that towel, and keep going. This is how you build a business, or anything, really, at least in my experience.

But once that thing is built, and moving, and growing, you're going to have to stop, reassess, and edit your methods. The only problem is that your business is not going to stop (or at least you'd better hope it doesn't!) long enough for you to do this. So, you're going to have to adjust and change gears while the train is already in motion.

Like many founders, I had a pretty fucking brutal learning curve in this area. It took me many years, and a series of systems that were the best solution I had access to in the moment, to finally impose a bigger, better system on this madness. And it's still a work in progress—and with our continued growth and evolution, yet more new systems will most likely be required, going forward. There's not just one system that saves the day forever. But when it actually starts working, YES, it feels good! When we first faced a real test and responded with calm, not chaos, I cried. More on that later.

For now, my point is this: The next time you encounter a problem that you think is a people problem, or even a "you" problem, pause there. This may be a problem with your process. Whip out your detective's cap and do your due diligence. At the same time, don't be too hard on yourself if the answers aren't immediately obvious, or don't present themselves to you all at once. I can offer a few suggestions, based on what I've learned the hard way, but in my experience, this process is never all buttoned-up and beautiful. It's raw and messy, and you'll be running while you're doing it. A helpful point to remember is that taking any action is a step forward, and often a source of useful intel that will make your decisions and approaches even better. There's always room to learn and tweak and grow—it's my preferred method.

Here are some of the questions and actions I wish I'd thought of:

- ☐ Pause, take a beat, and look.
- ☐ What does success look like?
- ☐ Have these expectations been clearly communicated?
- ☐ What's the first step of our process?
- ☐ When we've done it right in the past, what were the steps we took?
- ☐ Who are the key players in the process?
- ☐ Are the right people in charge of the right tasks?
- ☐ Do we learn from our recurring mistakes or do we keep doing the same thing over and over, expecting a different outcome?
- ☐ Are there any recurring coordination problems?
- ☐ Do we have the tools we need?

**Before:
It was all
hands on deck
to renovate
our HQ, circa
2015.**

Whether you're running a team or trying to get a book published, you need to look at your process. Obsessively document what you're already doing. Zoom in on the recurring hiccups. Then design better systems that circumvent these unproductive habits.

I learned this eventually. But even right then and there, in year one, I made a conscious commitment:

The shit storms will be a part of this whole adventure, and in order to keep growing and getting better, I'm going to have to be OK with this. I'm going to have my ass handed to me at the same time that I'm seeing some pretty snazzy articles about me that make it seem like H&B is this problem-free land of milk and honey. I need to be OK with the sometimes gaping distance between those two realities. I need to be OK with always, ALWAYS, taking ownership of the mistakes and moving forward. Sometimes I would make the mistakes, sometimes others would; there is no distinction between the two. I'd have to own all of it, and to show up, and to make it right—internally and externally, whether I liked it or not.

Now I had a mantra: *Always keep going. Always create forward progress.*

▲ **After: Our showroom, from an article in *Fast Company***

SPECIAL SECTION

Focus on What You Have, Not What You Don't Have

(How to Be Resouceful as F*ck)

LET'S TAKE A SECOND HERE to address a not-so-small elephant in the room. Dreaming first and worrying about details later sounds great—maybe it's even starting to sound doable—but how do you actually make it happen? Especially when you've got no money. The good news is that, most of the time, working with a budget actually means coming up with something fresher—and better.

When I lived in Mexico, and later when I was running H&B and the stakes were even higher, I always tried to think outside the normal path and come up with a solution to the problem, not just let the problem crush me. So from day one, I had to get extra creative, and not just go online and "order it" or hire an agency to "do the research" or "do the work."

Hedley & Bennett was born as a self-funded company. I started it in a house I shared with a bunch of roommates, each of us on our own life adventure. With my five hundred dollars in savings and three cooking jobs, I was making enough to not need to live on any of my early profits from my business. I also took to heart the wisdom of never spending more than I made, so I avoided debt like the plague, and I reinvested every extra penny back into the business. I kept my final day job for a year while building the company, before I dared to fully take the leap. I had to put in long hours during the week and even longer hours on the weekend, and instead of outsourcing or hiring someone to do whatever "it" was that needed to get done, I Googled it, read about it, asked friends, and did it myself.

Starting a new venture is going to be hard, financially and personally. There are no shortcuts around that reality. However, there are creative ways to stretch your dollar to get you an inch or two closer to your dream. These tricks are the Ellen Bennett way. They gave me a little bit of breathing room when I needed it. They ensured I had extra savings when I really needed it.

Barter (Use What You Have to Get What You Need)

People are often surprised when I tell them about how many things I've bartered for over the years. I can see their brain gears spinning: *you can do that?!* Hell yeah, you can do that. It's just a matter of being really honest with yourself about what you have to offer. And then, being courageous enough to ask someone to take your offering in exchange for the money they'd normally be paid. Sometimes they're not even giving you something—like advice—you'd necessarily pay them for. Doesn't it feel better to show someone you appreciate their time, expertise, and help by giving them something concrete in return?

Just take one of my mentors, Shane. He's the CEO of this huge, publicly traded auto parts company, which may sound worlds away from aprons (and it is). I met him several years ago, through some mutual CEO friends. This was after we'd moved into our HQ, and I invited him for a tour. While he was there, I immediately sussed out that he was good at all sorts of stuff that were not naturally a strong suit for me—like the super-detailed world of finance! I swallowed my pride and showed him my books, which were a bit of a mess. All I knew was everything was paid on time, we had no debt, and we didn't spend more than we made—the rest was really blurry. He was kind and patient and helpful.

My goal was to get enough face time with him to learn his mighty business ways. Instead of just asking, and taking, I offered him something I knew was an asset: my cooking. Not only that, but because I knew he was a big family man, I pitched him on coming over to his house and teaching his kids to cook. He and his wife loved the idea. It was so much fun. Not only did I get to know Shane and his family better than I ever would have at a stuffy business meeting, but he saw who I really was, and that helped him to give me better advice. The concrete knowledge he gave me helped me to set up more effective systems for H&B, led me to hire a part-time CFO, and literally saved me tens of thousands of dollars and at least as many headaches.

Things I've Exchanged My Skills and Assets For

- ☐ The pattern that launched Hedley & Bennett
- ☐ The financial advice that changed H&B's trajectory
- ☐ The amazing La Colombe coffee we offer to HQ visitors

When you're short on funds, think about what other assets or skills you have that people could want. There is more currency in the world than paper currency! My currency was my ability to cook. With a big smile, I offered my food skills in exchange for sewing patterns and financial advice.

And then, when I had buckets of extra space in my enormous H&B HQ, I traded an unused corner to the stellar coffee company La Colombe, so they could create their first LA outpost. They got an area for their LA staff to work and to train new baristas. And my staff, and everyone who visited the factory, got free coffee. This relationship could actually be described more accurately as emotional bartering—because we were essentially vouching for each other with this partnership. We were both saying to other people in the food world that we believed in each other enough to team up, even just in this small way. And we both gained exposure and squad members, thanks to the reach of each other's companies. When I'd become close friends with Jeni of Jeni's Splendid Ice Cream, we did the same thing—making her ice cream (and hugs) a complimentary treat during any trip to H&B HQ. People love surprises, plus, it feels good to join forces and offer your platform to someone, or a company, who's fighting the same fight as you—and on some tough days, this little boost of morale is a lifesaver (as is coffee and ice cream!)

Follow Through on Advice (and You'll Get More Help)

Oh, and here's the other thing: whenever Shane gave me sound advice—an article or a book to read, an overhaul to make at H&B—I ALWAYS did it as well as I could and as soon as I could. And then, I followed up with him to tell him how it had gone, and to see what task I should do next, to build on this knowledge or progress. By doing so, I showed him that I took his advice seriously. And I got him to take me and my business seriously, which led to more good advice. People are busy, especially successful people, and if they're generous enough to share their time and knowledge with you, there is nothing more disrespectful than simply filing the info away in a drawer and never doing anything with it. Plus, businesses and relationships are dynamic, and they grow bigger and better the more attention you give to them. Obviously, don't become a nuisance—read the interaction for how quickly it's reasonable to follow up, and with how much specific information. But I've definitely seen how fruitful a reasonable back and forth can be.

Make good use of what people offer, and they'll happily help you more.

Don't Be Afraid to Ask

Not to beat you over the head with a meat tenderizer about this, but here's your last friendly reminder: if you want something, go out and fucking ask for it. (I know, I know, for years of my life, I was the girl who was afraid to hear, "no." But I was also the girl who found a work-around by deciding to always offer something in exchange for my ask, which gave me the chutz-pah to do it.) Find your own way to push yourself beyond your comfort zone. Take the steps to make things happen in your life. It might require some patience, and some follow-through, but it could eventually lead to something great. Even if the person you want to work with doesn't need you today, keep showing up. Bring value to the table, and you just might get the opportunity to be a part of something special. I feel like sometimes we're too quick to demand and expect stuff before we've proven our-selves. Do your research to make sure someone is really worth aligning yourself with. Take your time. And then, take a risk. Offer something of yourself to someone you respect and admire, who feels a little beyond you. It just might pay off.

Do It Yourself

I'm a DIY gal, both out of necessity and because I have an innate, creative itch to make over the world. When I was little, I took it upon myself to redecorate our apartment. I went to Home Depot, picked up the neces-sary supplies, and got to work, painting every room in the house. Finding resourceful ways to create beautiful things has always been my MO, and

I applied this money-saving DIY attitude to creating the early days of the Hedley & Bennett headquarters.

Before our HQ became our HQ, it was a less-than-spectacular warehouse, but I saw potential. I saw colorful walls. I saw a big, communal kitchen. I saw a vibrant, beautiful space ripe for creating GORGEOUS aprons. What I really wanted was to craft a space for the community, where we could throw events. Of course, for me, gathering people together meant one thing: I needed a monster kitchen. As always, we had next to nothing to spend. So we slapped together what we could muster with IKEA classics, and by Vitamixing it—a term we'd coined, back in our last office, for when you want something, and then out of thin air, you have a situation present itself that enables you to get it; I'd wanted a Vitamix, and the next thing I knew, a TV show agreed to barter the kitchen gear they had for the aprons they wanted—which I had. And it included a Vitamix. Tadaaaa! *Vitamix*. This approach helped us to land a load of appliances. Our kitchen was stripped down in the beginning, but it was an instant centerpiece for food and fun times, and we used the shit out of that thing. We found creative ways to stretch our hard-earned resources to develop colorful, beautiful products and spaces. In turn, these products and spaces made us more money.

Even if you have previously been a little shy about rolling up your sleeves, getting in there, and giving something a try, it's never too late to start. The DIY method can still work for you. Do you eat out normally? Discover your love for cooking. Want to save money on your nonbusiness expenses? Teach yourself basic coding instead of hiring someone to build a website. Doing it yourself depends on your goals, your strengths, and what makes the most sense for your dream. You are more resourceful than you realize, and you don't always need to pay people to create things that you can make happen for yourself. Plus, the more your venture grows, the more you'll have to offer. Once we'd beautified our HQ, we were able to trade the use of this space to other companies that wanted to hold events there, in exchange for video of the events to be used on our social media, and lots of goodwill and community building.

Vi-ta-mix-ing / *noun* /
to have life present you with an opportunity
that might help you get something you've really
been wanting—in this case, a Vitamix—but only
if you recognize that opportunity and go for it.
Sentence: *I Vitamixed a Vitamix.* I wanted a
Vitamix. A TV show called, saying they wanted
aprons from us. They had no budget, but had
kitchen equipment. So, we traded aprons for
a Vitamix and a few other pieces of kitchen
equipment we needed.

Save, Save, Save

When our HQ, our sanctuary, was in jeopardy—Hi, Eviction Notice, we'll get to you later—I'd like to be able to say I had some next-level epiphany that allowed me to swoop in and save the day. But this was actually a case where having made some smart choices from the beginning paid off in a time of crisis. I'd always been very frugal with our piggy bank, and we had steady orders from our loyal restaurant customers. I actually had that rare thing in start-up land—a small nest egg. I worked with our finance people and made a plan. I could just bridge the gap so that we could hold on to the building, as long as we sublet a few corners of the warehouse out to other businesses, over the short term. But we had to hit all of our upcoming orders.

> **"Never spend more than you make."**
> Uncle Ted's advice rings in my ears every day since the beginning of H&B. Growing up with a single mom and limited resources, I learned how to be financially literate at a young age, both out of necessity and curiosity. The advice you're getting has been hard-earned by generations of financially savvy Bennetts.

Find a Way to Make It Work.
Be the Solution.

The best route is not necessarily the most expensive route. When I discovered a ten thousand dollar culinary school program in Mexico City, I leaped. This was the best way for me to get from point A to point B.

I started culinary school in 2006, after I'd been in Mexico City for about six months and already had my life pretty jam-packed, dawn to dusk. I slotted my classes into my day between my auditions and work shifts, recording all the details in the notebook I carried everywhere like it was a nugget of gold.

I was the only student with Spanish as my second language at the school, so I for sure stood out. And studying college-level courses in Spanish is a lot more complicated than ordering food at a restaurant. But it was a tight-knit class of about thirty students, and much like my final high school, I instantly felt right at home in this compact community of very different people from all walks of life. Some were older and already established in their careers, and were just seeking to supplement their existing knowledge. Some were younger and were learning the ropes to take over their family's establishments.

At the end of the day, there are financial realities and financial decisions that only you can understand. What I'm asking you to do is to utilize creative problem solving, so you can give yourself a shot before taking yourself out of the game. The amount of capital you actually earn and spend is only a fraction of the entire money-making equation. Think bigger, dream bigger, and take a leap of financial faith. You don't have to be twenty-four and single to be thinking of creative financial work-arounds, either. You just have to be honest with where you are, what you can do, what you actually need to do it, and what you're willing to do in order to make it happen.

6

They're Not Bumps in the Road. They *Are* the Road.

➡️ There legitimately is no secret way to keep your wits about you when everything is on fire—or feels like it's on fire. But the more times you go through it, the more comfortable you'll become with the uncomfortable.

After moving three times in three years, our growing company had to do it again in 2015. We'd outgrown my kitchen table, then the first four-hundred-square-foot closet of an office, the thousand-square-foot one, and lastly, the fifteen-hundred-square-foot add on in the same building. When our production manager saw a For Lease sign on the building right next door to our first very big, very legit manufacturing partner, I went to check it out.

The broker arrived and walked up with the keys jangling. He glanced over at me, looked me up and down with an expression that said: *you look younger than my teenage daughter.* But I chose my battles and just smirked right back at him. We went inside. It was a giant, cavernous disaster. Gloomy. Dark. Paint peeling everywhere. A total mess. As we walked around giant heaps of fabric, dilapidated machines, and wires that were haphazardly strewn all over the place, I loved it. I knew instantly—this was it. This was our future home . . .

As it turned out, our manufacturing partner next door also wanted a bit of room to grow, so I thought: *I'll get him to go in on the space with us. It will be perfect. We can grow together.* I had already been giving him sewing orders every week, and the numbers were going up. Their company was reliable, on time, and always did good work, plus they had been in business for many years. We autographed the papers together in mid-June 2015.

When my staff first arrived, they were quick to point out that the airplane hangar–size space was pretty awful looking.

"Ew. It's nasty in here."—One of my employees who shall remain nameless.

What they saw was the current reality in front of them. But where they saw grime, I saw potential. I imagined sunlight, brightly painted walls, potted plants, and dozens of beautiful aprons on display. A former screen-printing facility, it had too much paint where we didn't want it (over the windows) and not enough where we did (it was peeling away from the ceilings and walls). And there was a mountain of abandoned junk everywhere. But that was all fixable. Looking at the building, I was already imagining a space so large that it would inspire us to expand our own possibilities. It would help solidify an H&B world where chefs and cooks everywhere, from Michelin-star restaurants to people making roasted chicken for the first time, felt proud to wear our aprons, and this would be our physical representation of it!

First, we painted everything WHITE, so it looked fresh and crisp. We rented one of those industrial scissor lifts, scraping off the old paint, and redoing everything we could reach. Then, I got a recommendation for some guys to paint the rest—pro, but cheap. A winning (and necessary) combo. To liven it all up, my assistant Steph (a burgeoning artist) grabbed the keys to the scissor lift and started driving it around the space, hoisting herself up thirty feet, to paint some of my favorite inspirational quotes on the walls: "Everything's better with butter."—Julia Child; "If you can dream it, you can do it."—Walt Disney; and one of my own: "If the front door isn't open, climb in through the window," which we painted above a set of big factory windows on the outside of the building.

Lastly, I called on my trusty old contact, Dennis from Swing

Set Solutions. Dennis had built a swing for me in my old office, and now I had even bigger plans for him: Tree houses! Why build boring offices with drywall, when a double-level, playground-style tree house would do the trick—and be way cheaper than building new offices, too?

A proper internal renovation job would have cost forty to sixty thousand dollars and taken months, what with pulling permits, and bringing in a licensed contractor, etc. Instead, we got everything we needed with the help of one do-it-all fellow, Dennis.

When Dennis arrived for an initial walk-through, I pointed out where I wanted the two-story tree house offices to be. He craned his neck up to look, then shook his head.

"I don't know about having a two-story tree house in here," he said, flatly.

He was used to dealing with crazy parents, but he definitely questioned the operation at hand. We talked more.

"OK, we can do that," he said.

"But we need a zip line, too!" I said.

"That's going to be challenging," he said.

But after a little more thought, he was on board with this, too: "OK, we can do that."

Total cost: eight thousand dollars for two tree house offices, and the secret sauce for my HQ remodel dream.

We livened things up even more with a spiral yellow tube slide and an eighty-foot-long zip line; all of my Willy Wonka dreams come true.

Extreme Makeover: H&B Factory Edition

➤ When we renovated our 16,000-foot headquarters, we threw in more elbow grease than money, and the result was a magical Willy Wonka—style factory of fun. Some of the moments of inspiration that really made the space what it is today included:

Walking the grounds of the factory, dreaming up all it could be

Raw, American-made straps are one of the building blocks of our aprons.

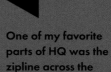

One of my favorite parts of HQ was the zipline across the showroom.

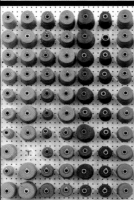

Our H&B factory, in LA, in full swing

Our Willy Wonka–style HQ, with office tree houses, slide, and test kitchen

The factory's test kitchen, for employee gatherings and community events with chefs

One day, about a year later, I was hosting a "welcome to the glorious Hedley & Bennett HQ" tour for a visitor when mid-performance, I glanced up to see my receptionist headed my way, looking extremely rattled. She knew not to blurt out whatever it was in front of our visitor. But she darted a significant glance toward a man in a suit standing at her desk.

"Hey, can I talk to you?" she asked me, shooting a scared smile toward the man.

"Sure," I said.

"Just give me a sec, OK?" I added to the guest in front of me.

He nodded and wandered off to get a closer look at the zip line and slide running through the middle of our warehouse. I was grateful for the distraction. I stepped a few feet away, yanking my receptionist into an impromptu huddle.

"Umm," she said slowly, swallowing hard. "Look at this."

She pushed a fat bundle of papers into my hands. I looked down and fell backward inside. We'd just been served with a thirty-day eviction notice. After everything we'd put into the H&B HQ, we were being kicked out of our hard-earned home sweet home for reasons unknown to me.

I knew there was a small risk when I'd decided to cosign a lease with our manufacturer, but I never thought it would end in such spectacular fashion: with him pocketing our half of the rent money, and failing to pay our landlord a dime for months, which led to our deposit—not to mention all of the rent we had already paid—disappearing.

Not only was he NOT in a position to pay back any of the money he'd taken, or otherwise contribute to a solution, his company was going under. ALL of his twenty-years worth of machinery, including some I owned, was being seized to pay his debt. I'd managed to get this far—five years in—without ever spending more than we made, with zero loans, and no outside investors. The company was 100 percent mine, and suddenly, so was the warehouse, and the massive amount we owed on the space. Even worse, I'd looked up to him, and clearly I'd put my wager on the wrong horse.

My fight-or-flight instinct kicked in. And like any self-preserving mammal, I fled—calmly. I excused myself from my guest, let him out of the building, and made my way to my trusty tree house. Now, here I was, a grown-ass woman, up in my tree house office, with a painted sign on the wall that read: "Clammy hands, full hearts, can't lose." I was wondering to myself: *How the fuck did this happen? How did I let this happen? What's wrong with us? With me? How could I ever let this go down? Fuuuuuuuuckkkkkkkkkkkk! I am losing!*

Was this the end of H&B? We'd be out on the streets, with no place to go as a business, right as we were heading into the fall and holidays, our biggest sales period of the year.

I had a choice: I could spend more time berating myself for going into business with an untrustworthy person and wallow in misery, or I could step back, acknowledge that circumstances had changed and my partner on the lease was no longer there to make this work, and figure out how to take back the steering wheel. In

The Entrepreneur's

→ Don't expect to avoid problems.

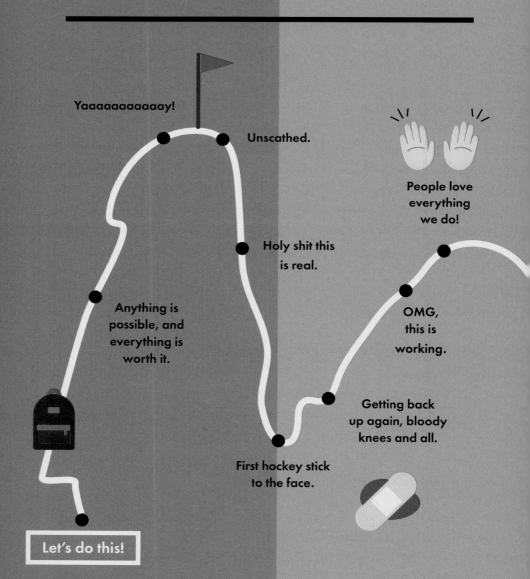

Yaaaaaaaaaaay!

Unscathed.

People love everything we do!

Holy shit this is real.

Anything is possible, and everything is worth it.

OMG, this is working.

Getting back up again, bloody knees and all.

First hockey stick to the face.

Let's do this!

Roadmap

Trust you'll get better at solving them.

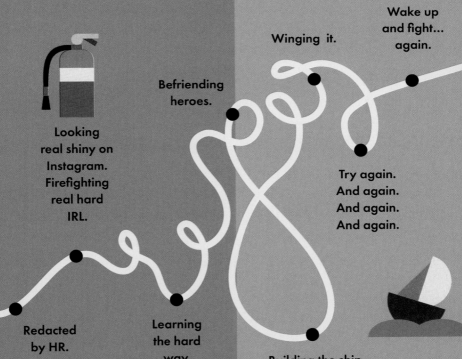

Wake up and fight... again.

Winging it.

Befriending heroes.

Looking real shiny on Instagram. Firefighting real hard IRL.

Try again. And again. And again. And again.

Redacted by HR.

Learning the hard way.

Building the ship as you're sailing the ship. And there's a hurricane. And a tidal wave. And the occasional tornado.

these moments of crisis that test your resolve as a human and leader, the measure of success is not what you did a week or a year ago, but how quickly you can start thinking like a problem solver, from exactly where you're standing today.

Wake up, Ellen, wake up!

OK, I needed to unfreeze and start thinking about what I had, not what I didn't. No one was going to rescue us—just our wits were left to help us—so I woke up and fought like hell.

First I needed to convince our landlady that I was actually an upstanding tenant. And some basic choices I had been making from the beginning had paid dividends. From day one, I had never spent more than I made, which was tough, because if we needed anything, we had to make the money first. Basic stuff, but it worked. I had also set aside 10 percent of everything we made, while reinvesting every extra penny in the company, and I'd barely taken any money in terms of a salary for myself. So I had a small but mighty savings account, and after reallocating money that we'd set aside for inventory for that year's holiday purchases, we decided to take those funds and apply them toward the first and the last months' rent we would now need to pay, along with the rent that hadn't been paid by our manufacturer, plus the new month ahead of us.

So there I sat, with our finance person in the little tree house, and made a plan. It wasn't perfect, but it was a way forward. And while analysis can be important, don't linger in that stage for too long—not making a decision IS actually you, making a decision, because the world will make it for you.

6 On-the-Fly Decisions I Made to Save the H&B HQ

1. Getting the necessary money by moving it out of savings, and by cutting all unnecessary expenses, LITERALLY THAT DAY.

---

2. Taking resources set aside for our holiday inventory purchases and use it to pay the deposit.

---

3. Not paying myself anything, until further notice.

---

4. Working out a payment plan with our fabric vendors for all of the materials we needed for the holidays, instead of paying for it all up front, like we normally did.

---

5. Getting everyone in the office in their Sunday best and persuade our ninety-two-year-old landlady, Peggy, to visit our WILLY WONKA FOR CHEFS playground, complete with ice cream and hugs.

---

6. Convincing said landlady to lease the 16,000-square-foot HQ to this twenty-eight-year-old (me), whose aunt had co-signed our first 400-square-foot lease.

I had never met Peggy in person, but I knew the building had special emotional significance for her because it had belonged to her dad. Well, that was something major we had in common—the warehouse could not have meant more to me if it was an extension of my flesh-and-blood body. I'd been pouring everything I had into it for months, and I was truly excited to show her how much love I'd given her space. So, just like I'd planned, I made an appointment with her. I hoped the building would speak for itself.

OK, cue Operation Save H&B HQ. At the appointed time of our meeting, a dignified elderly woman entered, craning her neck to take in how we'd transformed the space.

"Hi, Peggy! Welcome to the HQ," I said. "Look at what we've done with your building."

Please don't let it go away, I thought.

For the first few minutes, she let me show her all of the special details—the words of wisdom painted in large script on the walls, the pro kitchen, the slide! I may or may not have shown her the zip line, which our HR had advised me to stop letting people use. She walked slowly and silently, examining our handiwork. Finally, when I almost couldn't stand it any longer, she smiled at me.

"It's beautiful," she said. "You made it look so nice. My father would've been proud."

Yes! We'd made it over from dark and dingy, windows painted shut, to this light, airy, inviting paradise. We'd given it a soul and made it into something special.

"OK, you've proven yourself," she said. "The space is yours."

I sighed. I breathed. I allowed the heart attack to be deferred, at least for that day, feeling peaceful, knowing that we would still have our home.

That conversation taught me that even though the world can let you down with no thought for feelings, it will also reward you generously for doing the little things with integrity when no one's watching. And sometimes—just sometimes—it all evens out.

I also learned, yet again, that the road to success is not a one-way superhighway. Rather, it's a long one with hairpin turns, potholes, and speed traps, and sometimes it seems to take you backward.

● ● ●

NOT LONG AFTER ALL OF THIS HAPPENED, I watched as the logo belonging to our former manufacturer was painted over on the exterior of the building next door. He had been a big small business owner with a big dream, just like me. And just like that, it was as if his enterprise had never existed. Right around the same time, American Apparel—just down the street—closed its doors, too. That was a sobering reminder of how fucking hard it could be, even for companies with some serious miles under their treads.

But I don't regret for a second my decision to sign a lease with him. As I've learned during my years on the H&B high seas, sadly, not every solution or relationship lasts forever. There are chapters in the journey that need to end, and then you keep on going and leave them behind, but don't forget what you learned. I didn't have

How to Deal with Someone Who Is Upset or Angry With You Because of Something You Did (Whether You Agree with Them or Not)

☑ If you are mad, too, take a beat. Do not talk or react in that moment. Ask to step outside or even leave. Breathe. You are NOT thinking straight right this second.

☑ Don't ignore it or them. Acknowledge them, the issue, and their feelings.

☑ Do not respond by email or text. It is really tough to fix something fucked up in a texting battle or with an email cop-out. Get face-to-face, or at least on the phone. (This goes for most things, including firing people, or quitting a job—don't cop out!)

☐ Navigate their defensiveness and get them talking.

☐ Listen.

☐ Don't make excuses. Just listen and let them know you are listening. Say, "I hear you. I understand." Mean it.

☐ Pick one point you agree with and acknowledge it. "I can totally see how when I did X, I didn't handle it as well as I could have. That's my bad. Thanks for pointing it out."

☐ Say: "I'm going to work on that. Next time I'll handle it better." Mean it.

☐ If there's something you don't agree with, try to explain your side in a nonconfrontational way: "As far as Y goes, let me tell you where my head was at."

☐ Thank them for having this conversation with you. If appropriate, let them know you'll be sending a follow-up email that outlines what you talked about and next steps.

---

the money to rent the whole warehouse when I'd first signed the lease almost a year earlier. But by the time that lease partnership imploded, I had a plan for how we could afford the entire warehouse. So then and there, I signed the lease on a sixteen-thousand-square-foot building with our name on the side of it and rainbow walls to match. It felt like a new beginning to an already new chapter, and I was bruised and bleeding a bit, but still had some fight left in me.

So remember, you CAN'T play the game of life from the sidelines. You need to leap into life and LIVE IT. You will hit dead ends, roadblocks, potholes, shit storms, and a whole lot of other people's opinions about how you CAN'T do something (and sometimes your own head will chime in, too). But when you do, just know that all of this is a part of the journey and peel yourself off the ground, scratched up and all, and KEEP GOING.

You have everything you need to get unstuck. If you did it once, you can do it again. If you haven't done it once, you can damn well give it a try for the first time. It won't be perfect, but whatever happens, it will be better than you standing on the sidelines, thinking about it forever. Leap back in!

5 Things I Do When Life Throws Me a Curveball

(1) Don't hide from it—really look at the problem and understand what's occurring.

---

(2) Take a bath while I wallow in my own thoughts for a little while.

---

(3) Don't make impulsive decisions. Sleep on it. Respond in the morning with a fresh POV.

---

(4) Call any trusted friends who have been in similar situations. Have a sounding board you can talk to, but in the end, formulate your own thoughts and plan.

---

(5) Don't get too precious about it, once you figure out what to do. Your first reaction might not be the right one. Or you might have to change course once you know more. That's OK. Just make a start.

Stop,
Collaborate
&
Listen

➡ When I'm coming together with my favorite people, I want to do my favorite thing with them: make something brand new and wonderful.

That's exactly how H&B started, getting in there, elbow-to-elbow, with my favorite chefs, and cooking up an amazing new apron design, with direct input, one by one. I'd been coming to realize how much I loved this mode of creating—true collaboration between people who are melding minds and each bringing something unique and essential to the making table.

But as my team grew back at the HQ, and the apron-making machine of H&B started to get its legs underneath it, I happily began to lift my eyes to new kinds of collabs that could push our business (and myself) forward. Coming up as such a small, bootstrapped company meant that often my ideas were bigger than we could pull off, left to our own devices. But with the right copilots on board, I was sure anything was possible. So, I kept my eyes and ears constantly peeled, always on the lookout for the magic moments when my one and their one would add up to three.

That's how I got myself, and H&B, into a five-city goodwill tour in October 2016 with one of my new best friends and a constant source of entrepreneurial inspiration, Jeni Britton Bauer of Jeni's Splendid Ice Creams. I don't know who came up with the idea first, or if we dreamt it up at the same time, but it occurred to us that: *If bands can go on tour, why the hell can't an apron lady and an ice cream lady go on tour?* Plus, the country seemed like it could use a dose of goodwill at that moment.

Neither of us was probably going to do it on our own, but as soon as we each knew the other was on board, it was game on.

I flew to Columbus, Ohio, where Jeni is based. Starting there, we rolled through the south in our rented camper, with a few teammates in tow. The goal was to go to different cities we'd never been to, meet chefs, and spread the love. We'd hand out an RV-load of ice cream and aprons, every step of the way giving pep talks at schools, and leaving behind as many smiles as possible. We would build even more of a community in our wake, person by person, street by street.

We spent nine days in total visiting five different cities, including Louisville, Nashville, Atlanta, and Birmingham, traipsing through the region, gifting our wares, meeting our fellow entrepreneurs, hosting brunches, and sprouting new ideas left, right, and center. Just take our arrival in Louisville, where we leapfrogged into Chef Ed Lee's wonderful 610 Magnolia. It was the middle of the day, so the kitchen crew was busy, prepping for that night's service.

"We're here!" we yelled as we burst into the restaurant. Chef Ed was aware we were coming, but no one else was, and before those chefs knew what hit them, I was already saying "hi," looking at all of the delicious food they were prepping, and tying aprons on all of them.

"What's going on?!" they said, bewildered and excited all at the same time.

"Well, we wanted to surprise you. We're on a goodwill tour! And we brought you guys ice cream and aprons to make your day."

As I was adjusting straps and tying up backs, I was checking everything out, tasting food.

"Jeni, bust out the ice cream!" I called out.

"On it!" she said.

She jetted out to the freezer in the RV and hurried back, her arms stacked with pints of Brambleberry Crisp, Honey Vanilla Bean, and Boston Cream Pie.

A whirling tornado of pints and spoons, she doled it all out to everyone.

While they were kicking back ice cream by the pint, I was wrapping new aprons on people, making sure they got to try on a full range of fabrics and styles.

It was like a fucking circus of good feelings and beautiful flavors.

"I don't know what just happened, but that was amazing!" the chefs said.

And then, poof! We were gone. Back in the RV. On to the next spot! The only things left behind were aprons and ice cream and a lot of new friends.

On the one hand, it was this really absurd way to connect with people, but on the other, it was exactly what I'd always imagined, which was to build a mighty squad, by literally going chef by chef, restaurant by restaurant, street by street. And Jeni got it. She shared my dream. I swear my face hurt from smiling so much by the time I got back to LA.

● ● ●

THE NEXT YEAR, I wasn't thinking about anything but scrambling down a busy sidewalk in downtown LA to get to the panel I was about to be on at ComplexCon, an annual streetwear conference. All of a sudden, a woman stopped me, amid this crush of every type of streetwear kid you could ever imagine.

"Hi! Wait, are you Hedley & Bennett?" asked this super-friendly lady. "I'm from Vans. We've always wanted to do something with you!"

"Really?!" I said. "Everyone always says that we should do a collaboration with Vans, too. This is crazy."

A few months earlier, at an H&B brainstorming session, I had called out Vans as just the kind of rad brand I would love to partner with someday. And our marketing team said it was the number one requested collaboration. We stood there, basking in the cosmic coincidence that had slammed our paths together. (Talk about Vitamixing!) I mean, what are the fucking chances of that?

"I'm running to a panel," I said. "Can I give you my number?"

Laura surrendered her phone, and in proper Ellen Bennett fashion, I typed like the wind, putting in my name, and taking a picture of myself, so she'd know it was me. I saved my contact info, down to the email, phone number, and hell, even my birthday!

I made the assumption, right then and there, that this collaboration was going to get done. And not just in my head, either. I decided it out loud—with her. Much like when Chef Josef had told me that he'd met a woman who was going to make aprons for him, the opportunity was presented to me on the fly, and I leaped at it. I knew I would figure it all out later. The important thing was to grab the moment and go for it!

"This is so exciting," I said. "You don't even know how many people have wanted us to do a collaboration with you guys."

"Me too!" she said.

We hugged in the middle of the sidewalk, surrounded by a coursing stream of people, running into the conference. Then, I ran off to my panel.

I reached out later. I believe strongly that when you meet really smart, successful people in life, who tend to have everyone ask them for stuff, don't be that person. Instead, show them you value them by being giving, helping them, and supporting them in any way you can. *Empower this person who is typically hit up for everything.*

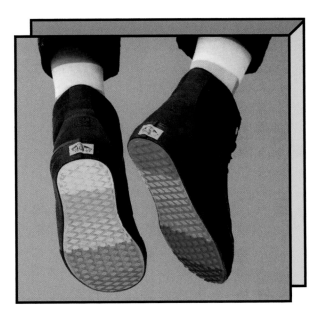

▲ The Vans x Hedley & Bennett collab shoe

How to Create Awesome Collabs

➤ LAURA AND I SET UP A CALL. We had a big brainstorming session, where we talked about all of the different fun things she was in the middle of doing. Just like with all of my collaborators, I made sure to really listen, and really be present in the moment, so I could glean areas where I might be able to leap in and help. And then, I told her all of the fun things we were doing. I could tell she was really listening. It was already very collaborative, and we hadn't even officially decided what we were going to do together yet. We were taking the time to get to know each other.

I really liked Laura. She was cool. She was smart. She was young. She was such an entrepreneur within Vans, and running a whole division of this massive company. I just knew: *We're going to be friends, because she's a good egg, this one.* Decision made.

How to Be Awesome to Your Potential New Collaborator

☐ **Start by offering something.**

☐ **Commit to getting to know them and their unique situation and challenges, so you can figure out how to be a helpful ally.**

☐ **Even if you're a small company just starting out, you always have something to offer: your time, energy, product or service, whatever contacts or social media presence you've already established.**

H&B was about to do our first-ever School of Hustle event, in partnership with Instagram, which was meant to be a high-energy, super-inspiring summer camp for entrepreneurs, where they could come to the factory, hear badass panels, meet kindred spirits, and of course, chow down on delicious food. I invited Laura to be on a panel at that, and she got to come to the office and see what Hedley & Bennett was all about firsthand.

So while building the bones of a work partnership, a friendship was born, too. We kept talking and listening, back and forth, keeping the ball rolling down the path toward an actual collaboration.

▶

The Vans x Hedley & Bennett ice cream truck at ComplexCon

Some Questions to Ask Yourself... and Them

☐ **What do you guys want out of this collaboration?**

☐ **What are your goals, as a company, and for this particular collaboration?**

☐ **What does success look like for you in this venture?**

☐ **Are you like-minded and are your goals aligned?**

☐ **Is each side bringing something unique and different to the table?**

☐ **How do we make the product or collaboration truly unique?**

It's important that you, as well as your collaborator, are able to answer all of these questions, honestly and clearly.

We started to have these mind-melding brainstorming sessions about a potential collab, where there was no such thing as a bad idea. It was just us, ranting and raving, about all the ways we were possibly going to do something, and what could actually get done. This is one of my all-time favorite things to do in life. When you're creating with others, you're no longer talking about reality. You're using your imagination to invent something totally new. I almost feel like I go into little kid mode, like how they can dream and imagine things with no restrictions or doubts.

My Favorite Tools for Brainstorming

- Good old-fashioned doodling on paper

- Paint markers on windows (the sliding glass door at my house is always packed with notes)

- Mood boards made from found images and components

- Pinterest images as inspiration

- Google slides, which allow you to dump your brain/all your ideas into one place

With Vans, it was a perfect opportunity. They were making a product (sneakers) that we didn't know how to make and weren't in the business of making. And we also wanted to be good partners, so we asked them: "What is something that's exciting to you guys that Hedley & Bennett does that we can build on together?" It turned out we had an audience that was very different from theirs—by teaming up with us, they were tapping into this chef space that's so unique. We had to do a shoe together.

How could we apply H&B's chef-driven professional eyeballs onto a product in the shape of a shoe? We changed how the inside of the shoe fit to the shape of the foot, for chefs who stand on their feet all day. We had an ampersand embroidered onto the back of the shoe. We really went wild and had the same rainbow of color that's painted on the outside of our building placed on the sole of the shoe. It was navy blue and looked low key, but when you flipped it upside down, and saw a whole rainbow of color, that was the reminder to yourself that no matter how professional you are out there, you should NEVER stop dreaming and doing and hustling and always having that extra pep in your step.

In September 2018, about a year after Laura and I had met, we launched our special sneakers. They sold out, which was a very exciting moment for us. But our collaboration didn't end there. In 2019 we collaborated on a second shoe drop, and this time we created a whole ice cream truck for the launch of the shoe at ComplexCon—the event where Laura and I had met so many years earlier. On the back of the truck we featured a quote I wrote out and then had made into vinyl that expressed our shared philosophy: "We created these shoes as a reminder of the dreaming, doing, building something out of nothing, gritty hustle that it takes to make dreams happen in the world."

Honestly, our collaborations have been some of my most joyous experiences at H&B and have resulted in some of the creations I'm proudest of.

I've also learned a hard truth, the uncomfortable way:

The Golden Rule of Collaboration
A collaboration only works if both sides bring something different to the table, and both collaborators genuinely show up, contribute, and deliver.

In the beginning, we said yes to pretty much everyone who asked us for an apron or the use of our space or our platform. Over the years, I've had so many people come to me with the same pitch: "We're such big fans of Hedley & Bennett, and everything you guys have done. It's so incredible. We'd love to do something with you. We'd love to have you host this event."

Of course it's gratifying to hear these kinds of compliments. And I like to help people. And the whole point of all the effort we put into the HQ was to create this amazing community center for our tribe. But what too often happened was we would end up being people's event planners, and hosting them in our space, and helping them to find people to come to their event. And, sadly, not everyone we did this for reciprocated. We're much more careful about who we team up with now. Time and energy are valuable resources, not to be squandered. So be aware, in business, that there will be lots of shiny opportunities that seem fun, but you have to ask yourself: Is it something you have the bandwidth for? Is your team able to help make this a reality? What else is going to get set back because you are spending time, resources, and effort on this? Is it going to move the boat forward in the right direction, or is it more of a distraction?

Once you run through some of these scenarios, then you should feel OK to say yes or no to certain opportunities. It took me years of yeses to learn to say no, and when you can finally say no, it turns out it can actually be a beautiful feeling.

H&B Collaborations

Williams Sonoma

Rifle Paper Co.

Joy the Baker

Oh Joy!

Richer Poorer

The Hundreds

Parachute Home

Topo Designs

(RED)

Madewell

Don Julio

Vans

8

GETTING OFF THE BIKE TO FIX THE BIKE

➡ One day in 2018, out of nowhere, I got an email from my CFO and head of HR, inviting me to meet for coffee at 7 a.m.

Both of them commuted from Orange County and usually started around 10. So I knew something was up. And I was nervous as hell.

As we scaled and grew, the soup of bad morale had been simmering more and more angrily. I'd been Tonka trucking along for FIVE YEARS at this point, and I was still ticking. We'd saved the factory, and we'd filled it with a whole bunch of new employees—bringing our sewers in-house—scaling our production accordingly. We'd leaped at new opportunities. We'd continued to build our squad, city by city, chef by chef. We'd reached the point where we were able to give our employees 401(k)s and health insurance. We'd implemented processes that cut down on the number of things falling through the cracks. And yet—we were still understaffed and under-resourced, still regularly selling out of core styles. Perhaps worst of all, my don't-ever-stop, 100-mph, fiery personality was getting the better of me in front of my staff. I just felt like we needed more experienced help, YESTERDAY.

I tried to fill gaping holes in our organization as quickly as possible, on the fly. So began the great consultant caper. During much of 2017, I did something I'd always been grateful I couldn't afford to do before—I threw money at the problem. I hired a series of part-time consultants and executives, hoping one of them would turn this canoe around before we went over the falls. Each had something to offer, and their own flavor of wisdom. Sometimes, though, their advice was great in theory, but in application it conflicted, or just didn't work. Some of these consultants were meant to be temporary. Others didn't last longer than a haircut, for a variety of reasons. When each said adios to H&B, they inevitably left behind half-implemented plans and processes, which the next person would come in and revamp. And so it went, creating what became a costlier, messier form of chaos.

Unlike many who had come before them, Niosha and Noelle

didn't rush to make a bunch of big changes. Yes, they jumped in and helped out and tweaked a few obvious issues, but mostly, they took the time to learn the lay of the factory.

I had some butterflies as I sat down with Niosha and Noelle for what we now call "The Intervention."

They got right to the point:

"First of all, we don't even know how you're still standing. It's been five years of you just running at full velocity, head down, trying to grow this thing, basically on your own. The fact that you've made it this far, by yourself, self-funded, with no outside resources, and no debt—it's a miracle that you're still alive. But that doesn't change the fact that something's got to give. There's a lot of weight on your shoulders, which is turning into pressure, which is creating a not great work environment. Are you going to let your company be full of people who are disgruntled about working here, or are you going to do something about it?"

There were certainly compliments in there as well. (They're both really pro at what they do and knew better than to machete my self-esteem, prior to dishing out the constructive criticism.) But they did have to download all of their observations about what was REALLY happening at H&B, and why people were upset. I sat there, I listened. I cried.

"You're right, something's gotta give," I said, sniffling through tears. "I'm tired. I'm frustrated, and I just feel like I'm out of bullets. Every day is a challenge, and it just feels like we aren't all rowing in the same direction."

3 Things That Were Happening in My Company (Some of Which I Didn't Know Were Happening)

① A lack of transparency in our books meant that I didn't know how solvent we were.

② There was a feeling of underappreciation, while also constantly having to weather a fire drill; I'd thought people would feel appreciated when I did things like give them 401(k)s and health care, but that didn't have the impact I'd hoped it would.

③ Some people didn't want to change, even when we were putting in new procedures, because it was easier to stick to "the way it had always been."

"Half the time I feel like you just need a hug," Noelle said. "But I don't know if you like hugs."

"I love hugs . . ."

With a laugh, we broke the tension bubble and got down to the nitty-gritty of what needed tuning up.

I started working, week in and week out, with a brand new executive coach on the very unsexy (but super important) task of interdepartmental communication and relationship building. She had already met with my staff members for individual one-on-ones.

I needed to work on how I managed and delegated to my team.

This meant taking a beat, instead of stopping to fix the problem immediately and involving everyone. No more trying to get all hands on deck to solve every problem. (Employees would run around like crazy, doing their absolute best, and with their hearts in the right place, but only adding to the disruption.) It meant talking to employees privately if there was a mishap, instead of in front of others. It also meant being much more direct about what I expected and when, and making sure employees checked in regularly and renegotiated if they weren't going to be able to meet their deadlines, so there would be fewer last-minute bad surprises. It meant more business, less emotion, and way more accountability all around. All of this allowed us to take the emotion out of our work, and have clear expectations—on both sides—of our roles. Mostly, my coach was teaching me to take a beat, especially when things got heated, and to look at things from a different perspective. As she pointed out: Your perception of something can be different from someone else's POV. And just because you're saying something doesn't mean that's what the other person is hearing.

KAPOW!

At first it was so hard. It felt like I was learning to walk and talk all over again. And it took months for the smallest shifts to happen. During those months, my coach would sit with me in my office and prepare me for every one-on-one meeting with an employee. It wasn't long before I had to have more difficult conversations.

Around this time, I saw the news that U2 was coming to LA. H&B at the time was a brand ambassador for the AIDS-fighting nonprofit, (RED), and we'd been honored to design a special apron for them, with proceeds going to the cause. And since U2 does a ton of good work with this group (Bono created it, after all), the organization gifted us some tickets. Great opportunity to boost morale, I thought! I bought two more, and I took a handful of people I wanted to thank for their work during the previous month, when we'd gone through a staffing shake-up.

The problem was that the rest of my employees didn't understand why they weren't being thanked. In fact, when U2 came to town, it got gnarly. I was getting a lot of shade from other employees who were rattled by the shake-up and felt like the concert invites were favoritism. One employee let her displeasure be known by acting up.

Even with the support of my coach and my high-up helpers, it took me a heartbeat to figure out what to do. Six days, if you wanna be exact.

Finally, I got that I was going to have to be the bigger person, be the CEO. So I texted her: *Hey, I'd love to meet up with you. Let's meet somewhere.*

So my unhappy employee and I sat down at a little spot to dig into some Thai food. I'd just come from a spin class, so my brain was firing on all cylinders. And I was staying on point by looping this coaching-style mantra through my mind: *I'm just going to listen. I'm going to listen to her as a human being, not as my employee.* Approaching it like that, I allowed the ego and emotions attached to our recent little dustup to get left in the car.

Instead of telling her something about anything, I started with a question.

"How are you doing? Where's your head at?"

She opened up like a bat out of hell, in the best of possible ways. In the midst of her honestly, sincerely telling me everything she was feeling, it became clear that she had misconstrued a bunch of stuff during the recent staffing shake-up. I didn't attack her for misunderstanding, or take it personally (which, hell yeah, is what I would have done before). Instead, I listened, taking mental notes of a few inaccurate details. I didn't breathe a word until she'd had the chance to say everything on her mind.

"I totally get where you're coming from," I told her. "I want to give you a little more context on how a couple of those things you were talking about actually worked."

Without any emotion, or a cement block of resentment on my shoulder, I provided her with more information. By doing so, I showed her the full landscape painting.

"Oh!" she said. "I felt like, before, you would've asked me to help, but you didn't. Instead, you just focused on the individual department. And you invited, specifically, only them to the concert, and I didn't understand why."

Work-in-progress Ellen took a deep breath and said, "I totally hear you, but again, I want to give you some context on how this actually happened."

By the time our plates were clean, she'd shifted her entire mindset, of her own volition, 180 degrees. She started marching forward, with me, and with our team. Plus, I got the positive reinforcement of weathering a sit-down that was out of my comfort zone, and seeing how it was so worth it. This inspired me to dare to be more vulnerable with employees in the future.

On the evening of this initial interpersonal breakthrough, I was getting prepped for all such conversations by my coach. Two years later, so many of these techniques have become the salt, fat, acid, heat of how I do business. For starters, not jumping down the throat of a situation, even when there's some obvious tension or bad feelings simmering. Instead, I try to take a beat to get clear on what's actually happening, and how it would be best to approach it. Sometimes I check in with my awesome HR person first, to make sure I understand all of the facets of the employee-boss relationship that are involved. Then I try to find some nonstressful alone time with

The Salt, Fat, Acid, Heat of How I Do Business

→ Shout out to our girl Samin Nosrat, for breaking down how we break everything down (and coining the expression "salt, fat, acid, heat.")

- ● **Collaboration** is a heavy dose of **salt**.

- ○ **Iteration** is the splash of **acid**. You gotta keep throwing on a little acid till you get the right dose.

- ○ **Willingness to learn** and never saying you know everything is the **heat**. You gotta grill, broil, bake, toast, and never stop learning how to manage the heat.

- ● **Stick-to-ittiveness** is the **fat**.

the employee in question, and always, always, always start by asking them to talk about what they're thinking or feeling. I listen, really listen, I ask for clarification, making sure I understand what's being said to me, and what's expected. By the time we've taken these steps for each and every point of contention, these conversations can take hours. They're always exhausting. But in the moment, I'm present, and focused on finding a positive outcome for the employee, for me, and for H&B. I'm not going to lie, these hard talks may get easier, but they don't get easy. And yet, this is why I'm doing all of this, to really connect with people—both my customers and my employees—and to hopefully make their lives better.

● ● ●

OF COURSE, WHEN IT COMES to people within the company, it's always a lot more emotional and painful than it is dealing with discontented customers, no matter how hard we try to shine on all fronts. Cutting ties has always been tough for me, maybe because I'd gone through so much early loss in my life, as a kid with VERY messily divorced parents, and then as an entrepreneur. I felt a desire to hold on to everyone, even when it had clearly stopped being in everyone's best interest. For instance, in the early years of H&B, if an employee didn't work out, I took it super personally—like I had failed as a human, like the atmosphere was crumbling and falling all around me.

It didn't make anything easier that leading up to the great intervention of 2018, demands were rushing at me like a fire hose to the face. Meanwhile, I had many incredible, loyal, talented, employees to help. But almost all of them were kids like me, who'd come on board early because they'd cared more about the adventure and why of the job, than their compensation. I'd known we needed more assistance, even before anyone had pointed it out to me. But I was also still running—and harder than ever—now that I had more responsibilities in and outside the factory.

Once we started overhauling me, via my coach, and overhauling H&B, via a personnel reconfiguration, things got real in a way they hadn't before. I acknowledged that I couldn't just shine my way through any situation, or pull off last-minute miracles in the nick of time, like I had in the early days of H&B. I needed new kinds of help, and I needed to actually embrace the process that would allow this to happen.

We stopped running long enough to assess every person in the organization and whether or not they were a good fit—for the company, and for their role within it. We did something that would have caused me heart palpitations before. We laid out what the next years of H&B were going to look like and gave people the opportunity to decide to recommit to its future growth and the next chapter of change, or to say "it's not for me," and form a transition plan. And we had to make a few strategic changes of our own within our staff. Even with all of the extra support I had at the time, this was still really hard. But I came to see the wisdom in the fact that, sometimes, it really is best for everyone involved to help an employee transition onward.

Even though I'm not nearly as emotional about the process as I used to be, I still feel uncomfortable when I'm in the thick of it. But, now, I accept that it's just part of doing business, much like how you also have to streamline your processes and your habits— some people are a snug fit and some people aren't, and that's OK. I've found that if I know it must be done, it's best not to avoid it, or put it off. But I also don't do anything in a moment of heightened emotion. Breaking the news that an employee isn't working out has to be planned and choreographed as carefully as making a new hire.

My life improved dramatically when I realized that while some people are worth going to the ends of the earth for, business is business, and friendship is something I personally had to separate from business, along with emotion and taking things personally. Lots of really great people have come through the H&B doors, done their part, left their mark, and moved on, and that was the natural course of business—few were going to care as deeply as I did.

As my coach had said to me: "Your business is like a bus, and it's on a long journey, so it's only normal to have people getting on the bus and off the bus at different stops." Normalizing that, and allowing space for people to grow and evolve, and then also to leave, were just parts of the journey. It didn't make them, the company, or me any less. It was just a part of the path forward. Now, I'm OK with that, too.

9

Commandeer Your Copilots

➡️ **From the time my parents divorced when I was a little kid, I vowed I was going to be my own driver in the car of life, and never have to depend on anyone for anything.**

For most of my life, I was a self-guided fire hose, only with a warp speed setting. Pushing and scratching and scrapping my way through my teens and twenties and the early days of H&B, I'd used what I knew, made up the stuff I didn't, failing spectacularly, but willing myself to always get up to try again, always pushing my dream forward.

It worked great, until it didn't.

I had reached this weird, sometimes uncomfortable place where I was the boss. It was my responsibility to protect my team from the problems and growing pains at H&B, so they could focus on their jobs. I was also the source for most of the creative juice, and while that was one of my favorite parts of the job, we only have so many ideas at our brain tips before needing to occasionally do something to refill the well.

I didn't realize it at the time, but I was stuck in survival mode, and the big picture was suffering—in my company and in my life. I've seen firsthand how easy it is to get stuck in old ways of thinking and being, without realizing that they no longer match our environment or circumstances. That relentless drive that helps you to leap into the unknown, persist when you can't see a light at the end of the tunnel, and materialize solutions where other people see problems comes with a dark side: Sometimes you can't stop. And sometimes you're not very good at accepting help or input from others. When, really—as I was about to understand in all new ways—teaming up with like-minded badasses who have strengths in areas that you don't will only inspire your creativity, push you to new vistas, and help you to grow.

Even once my staff had expanded, so that we had way more skilled hands on deck to get things done and hit our deadlines, and were all set up at our newly marvelous HQ, I was still in pedal-to-the-metal mode. But I was discovering that, thankfully, there were a few cherry-picked people in my life who knew just what I was going through—some fellow dreamers and doers, who I'd been collecting along my journey without even realizing I was doing it. We were just kind of drawn to each other, like gum to a tennis shoe. And, more and more, as I struggled to keep my arms around the increased heft of H&B, I found myself flipping to their numbers on my speed dial.

I'd already seen how my own day-to-day existence had gotten a whole lot better, about a year into H&B, when the designer Joy Cho, of Oh Joy! stopped by my office with her daughter. The plan was for her to design mother-daughter aprons and pen a piece about my aprons for her blog. She would later become one of my closest friends and a bridesmaid in my wedding. I found I was able to unload at length about all kinds of headaches that only a fellow entrepreneur could fully comprehend. She got it. As she became one of my first and best sources of advice during all kinds of shit storms, it dawned on me how lonely I'd been for people who knew just how real the struggle was—who knew how exhilarating and terrifying and exhausting it felt when every penny came out of their pocket, and every decision had to pass through their heads, and sometimes, somehow, the failures felt like they outweighed any ounces of success.

I began to be much more aware of who I was surrounding myself with, and I cultivated my crew. Whenever I'd meet an amazing entrepreneur out there, who seemed to get the kind of things I might be going through, I'd stick myself to them like extra-strong Velcro. Soon, I'd amassed a crew of founders, including Jeni Britton Bauer of Jeni's Splendid Ice Cream, Bobby Kim of The Hundreds, Chelsea Shukov of Sugar Paper, Alli Webb of Drybar, Ali Cayne of Haven's Kitchen, Clare Vivier of Clare V., Christina Stembel of Farmgirl Flowers, and Iva Pawling of Richer Poorer. And, there it was, a lifeline of fellow founders, many of whom were at different stages of the process than I was, which could be super helpful. I didn't even think of our conversations as business building, because we were having so much fun and connecting on such a deep level, but I definitely learned so much from them.

> **Find like minds, who are also further along on their journey than you are. They will make you think larger and push you out of your comfort zone, because they show you what's possible. Share where you are in your journey, and then listen intently when they share their stories. There's so much to learn from people who've already done it.**

The One Who's Walked in Your Shoes

Who in your life just gets it? In their presence, you feel relieved and understood. You can put down your defenses and be vulnerable. You don't have to sell them on your struggle or explain why things aren't working out. They just know. These people are great allies to have on your speed dial #1-800-HELLLLLLP!!!!

I fell in love with my now-husband Casey because he's always been the calm to my storm, and yet creative as hell, and on top of that, he has epic listening skills. In the early days of H&B, which happened to be the early days of our relationship, I would often make use of my two secret weapons: Casey and our bathtub. Night after night, I would sprawl in the sudsy water, bawling my heart out. Casey sat on the outside of the tub and listened to me cry about whatever happened that day or week. Finally, I'd be all cried out and ready for bed. Casey coached me through many a meltdown, but more than anything, he let me exorcise all the thoughts and feelings that'd been broiling inside me all day.

Incidentally, he happens to also give really good advice. Casey is a creator. He'd founded and run *GOOD* magazine for more than a decade when we met. Like me, he could look at an empty space and envision myriad possibilities. And so I didn't have to explain myself to Casey or sell my vision, or myself, to him. He just got it. And since I'd been "on," nonstop, in the service of H&B for the past year, such instant synchronicity was a massive relief. I was like a fire hose of

> Who in your network can offer advice in difficult times? Who can you turn to when things go sour? Those are the relationships you need to nurture.

ideas and energy with no off switch, and he was like an idea vending machine, always standing by with the perfect concept or fix.

What you will most need from your network, and will come to depend on, is support.

With H&B's growth came all new challenges. Compared to the early days, I was chewing on way bigger opportunities and questions, which would directly impact the company's future. But most days, I was already so busy leading the charge, while taking on the full hurricane-level gale of issues that went with being CEO, that less immediate issues often got pushed to the bottom of my to-do list, which meant they never got dealt with.

And then, in early 2017, just when I was stretched as thin as fruit leather, I got exactly what I needed, even though I didn't know I needed it. I connected with another young founder, Christina Stembel of Farmgirl Flowers, based in San Francisco. We hit it off right away and made a vow to stay in touch. In these cases, especially with two busy-as-hell CEOs, it can be hard to keep your word. But, as you already know, I'm a big believer in holding onto the good

Entrepreneurs Ellen Loves

➤ I've always learned by doing and watching and jumping in to help others do, while asking a million questions. It's taken an army of helpers—all the people who have assisted me with advice, expertise, and their most precious asset: their time. Here's the crème de la crème, who told or showed me something that has informed or changed my approach the most.

My abuelita, Isabel (or Chabelita, as we called her)

As a kid, I got schooled by watching her sell clothes door-to-door in Tampico, Mexico. Everyone always welcomed her, this little spark plug of positivity. It wasn't what she was selling. It was the relationship she forged with every one of her customers. It was how good she made them feel.

My Uncle Ted
Owner of Tom's Toys, with three locations in California

One of my first jobs, when I was sixteen, was wrapping gifts at the Beverly Hills store during the holidays. He is how I want to be in business: fair, trustworthy, farsighted. He plays the long game, building relationships for the long haul, and earning people's trust to the point where they know that a handshake deal with him is as good as gold.

He gives great advice, like: "All that you can do is the best job that you can do, and then, always be proud of what you've done."

Chef/co-owner **Michael Cimarusti**, and co-owner/ general manager **Donato Poto**, Providence

Not only did they teach me to take a chance on people by letting me cook in their two-Michelin-star restaurant. But by being a one-two punch of perfection that feels graceful, they showed me the importance of putting the utmost, genuine care into every detail. By doing that, and being the best at it, you'll inspire your employees and transform your customers' experience because you strive to be number one, every day.

Chef Josef Centeno
Owner, Lazy Ox, Bäco Mercat, Orsa & Winston, Bar Amá, Amá Cita

Chef Josef taught me the power of saying yes by hiring me with zero experience and being Apron Squad Member #1. He educated me about how to get anything and everything done, through his own lack of ego and incredible work ethic. He's the perfect blend of humility and grit, worth emulating.

Dana Cowin
Longtime editor of *Food & Wine*, author, radio host

It was a huge coup for me when Dana championed H&B, and even more special when she became a friend. Another monster talent I've learned from. Watching her in action, I've absorbed the value of curiosity, and the merits of leaning in to experience and having a constant passion for learning.

Martha Stewart
Author, TV personality, entrepreneur, icon

I'm not gonna lie, it was a big deal when the boss herself outfitted the staff at all her Macy's cafés in H&B. She did one better by giving me this real-deal advice: Grow your dream as big as you can, and as hard as you can, and for as long as you can, until you can't grow anymore on your own. Hold onto ownership of your business for as long as possible. Then, and only then, partner up.

Martin Howard
Founder and CEO of Howard CDM, restaurant development and construction

I met Martin when we both rode our butts off at Chefs Cycle, an event to end hunger. I finagled my way into shadowing him. What I learned is that uber successful people cram in so much, make decisions faster, and always prioritize what really matters (family, philanthropy, results).

Marty Bailey
Chief manufacturing officer of American Apparel

When we landed the HQ and were setting up our sewing floor, he gave us all of the technical advice we needed to do it properly. And by observing him in action, I learned the value of the simple but timeless basics: Always say, "Please," "Thank you," and "What do you think?" Good manners go a long way.

Chef Jonathan Waxman
Chef-owner of Barbuto (NYC), Jams (NYC), Brezza Cucina (Atlanta), Adele's (Nashville)

Much like Chef Cimarusti, he taught me about going the extra distance to achieve excellence. I always saw him as so serious about the quality of everything he did, but also as a real ally, even from my earliest, scrappiest days. Every time he opened a new restaurant, he included me. I saw how he mentored so many cooks (and me) by giving us the opportunity to fail, but we never wanted to let him down, so we never did. And once we'd earned the right to even more responsibility, he always gave it to us.

Chef Jonathan Benno
Formerly of The French Laundry, Daniel, Gramercy Tavern, Per Se, Lincoln Ristorante, currently chef-owner of Leonelli Focacceria and Leonelli Taberna

I learned from observing Chef Benno that there's no such thing as an overnight success. It's all about working hard, learning, trying, growing, evolving, and pivoting. And, always, it's about giving back. He is a great connector within the food world, and he's shown me how gratifying that is.

Chef Marc Vetri

Chef-owner of Vetri Cucina, Pizzeria Vetri, founder of the Great Chef's Event to benefit Alex's Lemonade Stand Foundation

As with many of the other chefs who've mentored me, Chef Vetri has a great deal to teach about excellence and hard work. But what I really took from him was the importance of giving back through philanthropic efforts, and not just by donating money, but also time and heart. When I saw how busy he is, in addition to having three kids, I said: *There's no excuse for not doing more.* It's been our great honor to donate the aprons for his events every year since the beginning of H&B.

Jon Levine

Our consultant turned CMO and advisor

He came in, believed in H&B, and worked his ass off, side-by-side with me, to implement change and bring professionalism to so many aspects of H&B. He was a fundamental part of our journey from our preteens as a company to growing up to the next phase. When things seemed impossible, he always helped us to find a way through it.

Denyelle Bruno

President and CEO of Tender Greens, formerly oversaw Drybar and launched the first Apple stores

When I was striving to master the HR ropes, she taught me how to firmly but kindly let an employee go, which is hands down one of the hardest parts of being a boss. Mid-COVID, when it felt like the world was ending, I called her, and she said: "You have to be a leader right now. You're not asking people for suggestions. You are telling them exactly what needs to get done. What they need from you now is a leader who gives direct orders on exactly what you need to do to start making these changes. Now. Stop talking about it and start doing it."

eggs I find out there. Plus, looking back, I think we both were in need of just this kind of connection and the fruits it could bear.

She had been mulling over the idea of renting a house for the weekend, as her own private mini-retreat/strategy session. And she very generously invited me along, as well as another founder and one of my best friends and favorite people, Chelsea Shukov of Sugar Paper. We all brought what we had to offer. Christina provided the house and made it gorgeous with fresh flowers. Chelsea brought bounteous amounts of amazing paper products from her company. I packed my own personal larder and cooked for everyone, plus I threw in some of the giant oversized Post-its I love so much for getting down all of my ideas where I can actually see them. We arrived late Friday night and left Sunday afternoon. But we managed to cram a ton of amazing brain dumping and storming into those forty hours. Even though our companies were in majorly varied areas, and at vastly different stages of growth, we figured out the best way to support and be of service to one another.

By the end of the weekend, we'd each done a deep dive. We'd set our top priorities for the year ahead, listing them all. We'd set specific revenue goals, also writing them down. We'd questioned each other, in order to investigate what needed to happen to make these benchmarks possible. We'd written everything down, for accountability throughout the year, and so we could bring it to our next retreat, which we did the following year. I still have my sheets from both sessions, and they were a great source of inspiration and focus for the kind of big-picture planning it can be hard to get to amid the nitty-gritty of CEO life. These talks were also incredibly healing. Sometimes it's easy to feel alone when you're in charge of something. And it's just so helpful and galvanizing to spend time with people who know EXACTLY what you're going through. Plus, it's a great way to share specific resources.

I have Christina to thank for giving me the idea to do a retreat in the first place, and then for organizing everything. And both weekends that we put together were pretty fucking amazing. But here's the thing, it doesn't take a fancy Airbnb or a former professional cook slinging food to make your retreat next level. All you have to do is to lock yourself up for the weekend, with at least one fellow dreamer and doer, and hunker the fuck down. Don't get distracted by social media, or ordering pizza, or even any of the current day-to-day demands of your business. Instead, zoom out from the trees, and actually focus 100 percent of your thoughts and creativity on your big-picture needs and future plans. You could do it at your friend's house. You could do it in your backyard. Don't focus on what you don't have. Focus on what you do have. And don't make the excuse that you don't have enough time. As a friend always used to say: "If you want something done, give it to a busy person."

What I learned from these retreats was valuable on so many levels. For starters, teaming up gave me valuable moral support. It reminded me to not for a second think about feeling bad about myself for any places where I'd fallen short. Sometimes on this journey, it's easy to think you're alone, especially when you're captaining the ship. There had been so many moments when I'd thought: *Why is this so fucking hard? Why am I struggling with this? Is there something wrong with me?* But here were these incredible women, who were going through some of the same challenges. Right there, I saw that many people are fighting the same fight as you. Maybe you just don't know it, until you stop and look around for them.

It also helped me to grow in ways that my normal business life just didn't allow time or space for. It pushed me to new places and inspired my creativity through the examples of my fellow founders, and the many ways they upended my perspective with their own out-of-the-box thinking and next-level problem-solving skills. Remarkably, even though we were all superdriven speed racers, there was no competitiveness. I left feeling more inspired to work even harder and to push even further, just like they were doing in their lives.

• • •

SOMETIMES, A MENTOR'S OR PEER'S value add might be as simple as helping you realize what you already know. Or making you feel less shitty about yourself. Or reminding you of the larger goal. Or telling you how math works. Mentorship takes many different forms. It may be able to help you in ways that you can't even predict yet.

I think it's really important to remember that mentors aren't just for newbies starting out. At every stage of life, there are always new challenges to be conquered, and fresh knowledge to be gained. I have been astounded how, again and again, the perfect person always seems to come into my life at just the right moment to give me the advice I need. (Well, I'm not shy about getting face time with these folks, so that's a big part of it, but the timing is still remarkable.)

In 2019, I was wrestling with a big-time decision that I'd kept kicking down the field since founding my business in 2012—whether or not to take on outside investment money in order to grow the company beyond what I could do on my own. I met with a handful of the crème de la crème of the business world—some truly brilliant, inspired, successful people, who had all sorts of exciting, interesting visions for H&B. I took it all in. I talked to Casey. I chewed on the choice with many of my mentors, inside counsel, and all of my fellow entrepreneur friends. But I still wasn't near crystal clear on what was best for the company, for my employees, or for me.

And then, I met Rochelle Huppin, a chef and entrepreneur, like me, who'd founded a chef gear company, Chefwear, in her twenties, like me! Our experiences were so similar it was uncanny. When we sat down together for dinner, it was like we went into the Matrix, and suddenly, I could see the questions I'd been noodling on with all new dimensions and perspectives. It wasn't that Rochelle's advice was better than any of the excellent tidbits I'd already gathered. But as I learned firsthand, when someone has walked in your shoes and knows EXACTLY what you mean and what you've been through, there is just such a deep feeling of satisfaction and calm. Like, FINALLY, someone gets it, gets me, in a way that no one else on the planet really can. And because she'd been running her business for three DECADES, she had some major wisdom to drop on me.

During our first sit-down she said: "If there's one thing I can do for you, it's to not let you make the same mistakes that I made. What's done is done. But you can adjust your own path into the future. There were so many times when there were opportunities for me to make choices or take big leaps. I didn't do them, because people told me otherwise. I have regrets over that."

One of the most important gifts she gave me was to get me out of my own sandbox and open my eyes to just how many people are out there. I realized I'd mostly been whipping around in my own little world, while there were so many different people operating in different worlds. And that I should never be satisfied with what's in front of me without fully making sure I've explored every alternative first.

Rochelle never told me what to do or how to think. And my coach had drilled it into me that you can get advice, but you can't outsource your thinking. I knew the choice about outside funding was mine and only mine. It was a lot of pressure. Rochelle fit that sweet spot of someone who really got me, who listened to me, but also challenged me. Relationships like this are also the most rewarding part of everything we're trying to accomplish in life. When I survey the battlefields of H&B, I chalk up so much of my resilience to the fact that, when situations arose that I COULDN'T handle on my own, I had a pile of smart, experienced peers to guide me through to higher ground. And, as with everything else in the universe, there's no end to the growth and expansion you can welcome in this area. I'm still meeting and befriending new copilots, constantly. I'll never stop, because the adventure is always better together.

10

TRUST

➡ Your dream is your baby. HOWEVER. Every parent is working toward being able to take off the training wheels.

The day I left the office at 6:30 p.m. was one of the best days of my life. Especially because it wasn't just any average workday. It was Black Friday, which is like the Olympics in retail—the day after Thanksgiving, when most retailers have massive sales, do massive numbers, and launch their mad dash into the holiday rush. And to say that past Black Fridays had been rocky would be the understatement of the century. So, to have all of the hard work, humble enthusiasm, tough conversations, and big-picture collaborations come together on this day of all days was just incredible. Not that everything was perfect, mind you, but for the first time, maybe ever, it finally felt like we were at least running in the right direction.

Through a whole lot of trial and error, I've come to realize that all of the upgrades you make in a company only work if you trust the people doing the work on the ground. Stepping back and letting other people do what they do best is crucial for the whole team's success. H&B is my baby. I have ice-axed my way up the side of a mountain to keep it alive at times, as its primary caretaker for more than half a decade. So it's tempting to continue to be involved in every little thing pertaining to it. But in the past year and a half, really, I'd come to accept that as it's grown up, I physically can't, shouldn't, and will not try to micromanage it all. Trying to do everything, or be involved in everything, will only keep the focus away from the areas that I do best and that really matter for me to tackle. And it would also prevent the other members of my team from growing into their roles and landing what's expected of them. They're at HQ to add their special sauce, perspectives, and own work to the mix. The most helpful thing I can do now is to support them by having smart people leading every area, trust them, get them what they need, plant the vision, help them to see the full picture, and then, get out of the way, while letting them feel empowered to: own it, do it, crush it.

This was a very big self-awareness moment for me that took six years too long. When I finally realized all of this, it fully punched

Growing Up:
How to Set Up Team Members to Succeed

→ After plenty of trial and error, we've found some ways to ensure that employees are given what it takes to help them thrive at H&B:

☐ **Onboarding is key.** When someone new starts, we show them a deck we put together that walks them through what H&B is all about and what we stand for—it really takes the time to teach them about the company, what we're doing, and our deeper why.

☐ Each department has a designated manager who keeps an eagle eye on things, which helps everyone to know their lanes, and enables accountability check-ins to happen. It also means employees have a direct avenue for communicating their needs.

☐ A ninety-day plan is put together for each new person and their role, and it shows how their position affects and contributes to what the whole company will be doing, too. Weekly one-on-one check-ins with managers help everyone to keep their expectations out in the open and to make sure we're keeping shit straight.

☐ Our HR maestro makes sure any tough situations or conversations are handled in a neutral, professional way. When something goes wrong, it's more about what needs to happen differently than about the person who maybe didn't meet expectations. We talk it out, we document, we come up with a solution that is amicable, and then a PIP (progress improvement plan) is put in place.

☐ The weekly progress report is a real-time summary of each day, gathering up customer feedback and keeping track of what needs to happen, so the managers and I always have our fingers on the pulse of our squad and can spot any problems early.

---

me in the face . . . in a good way. This WAS the way forward, as a team, NO LONGER a one-woman band. This epiphany happened, and then I really had to start mindfully letting things go. I still had to pause before I instinctively wanted to jump in and fix things all over the place, but eventually, I learned (and will always be learning) to instead take it to the right person to get it fixed. A business is a living, breathing ecosystem and it takes time and nurturing to grow it, but it takes letting it go to let it become what it's destined to be—at least this was the case for H&B and me.

A perfect example of all the gears and pulleys working in harmony—with just the right systems and people in place, finally—was that mythical, magical Black Friday in 2019. By this point, seven years and a thousand skinned knees into the H&B journey, a lot of the pieces were in place. We had awesome designs and products. We had a devoted squad. We had streamlined systems (and backup systems, in case the primary ones failed). We had a cherry-picked team of devoted staff members who wanted to be there and knew what they were there to do. And, given some of my past tales of woe, you might expect this to be the moment when I insert a giant BUT and start describing how it all crumbled because of some oversight or faulty logic.

For starters, we didn't have just any system in place, we had what for me had been like the holy grail of structural accomplishments: an ERP (enterprise resource planning) system. Ever since I had heard about this integrated software system, I'd wanted one. It was like a big brain that hooked up not only to a company's inventory, but also to its QuickBooks, and its shipping, and its Shopify e-commerce platform, and its suppliers, and actually controlled our costs, so that there was a real-time view into what was coming and going on all levels. As nerdy as it sounds, one of my own personal North Stars was having an ERP system that was up and running, and for holidays no less. It meant that for the first time, we'd know what the hell was going on, inside and outside the building, during the busiest time of the year.

Not to mention that this was the finish line of what at times had felt like a technology wild goose chase. I had hired and fired any number of consultants who advised in this area and investigated sooooo many companies who offered different systems. And we'd even test-driven a few systems that hadn't been a good fit for

When you are bootstrapping a company, you don't spend more than you make, so if you want something, you've gotta earn it. If you need to buy a computer or a laptop or specialized equipment or an ERP system, you've got to find that money first.

us, which was a headache squared. But I knew that big, successful companies had ERP systems, and I had every intention of being a big successful company, and so to scale, we needed one, too.

And now, we had one and it was up and running. Hallelujah!

Next up was to test our mettle against Black Friday, with the ERP now in our toolkit, and all the other endless hard-earned improvements we'd pulled off over the years, including all of the care we'd put into HR, so we had the best people, trained properly, to use all of the tools.

It was amazing, even better than my wildest dreams. We knew when packages were landing. We knew when supplies were arriving. The ERP system actually notified us when a product was down to 50 units. At that point, an alert was sent, so our preproduction department (which we actually have now) could proactively start sourcing materials for reorder, before we even needed them. Whereas, in days of yore, we wouldn't have even known there was a crisis until a week later, when our larders were bare and we had Christmas orders to fill, pronto.

Over the years, there had been so many moments when I had leaped, feeling confident that I was doing what was right for the company and for my employees. And plenty of times, I had eaten it, hard. But this wasn't one of those cases. And it wasn't just the ERP system, either, although that was huge. It was the employees. And the social media platform. And the strategic partners. And the amazing living, breathing apron squad that was now stretching its arms around the entire world. All of this was finally coming together. Even though it had been a windy, complicated path to figure out all the different pieces that the company needed to grow up and to be a bigger kid, it had been the right type of growth, at the right pace. And we had hung in there, through the trials and the tribulations. And along the way, we as a company had grown so much more capable of handling the challenges as they arose, even if they still hurt. I knew I'd survive this Black Friday, whatever happened, and more. Even more important, I knew H&B would survive, too.

Although we doubled our orders from the previous Black Friday, we actually stayed on top of demand. My muscle memory definitely kicked in when I saw how busy we were. The HQ was noisy with people, scrambling around, getting stuff done and coordinating their workflow, plus the crash of boxes being packed and stacked. I helped out a bit in shipping—tying bows on some of the orders—but every time I offered to jump in, more often than not I heard the same thing:

"No, we've got it," my team said. "We're good on this."

I stood there, hovering, wanting to get involved, even though they had it covered.

Finally, I stepped back and trusted them, even though packing boxes during holidays had been part of my role for years. For the first few seconds, it was uncomfortable, because it was new. But then it felt really great, because this was the culmination of everything we'd all been striving for, and it was actually working!

And even better, now that I wasn't in the weeds of the details of the business, which were being handled by my team, I saw where I could actually be even more valuable. As I stood there in the shipping department, instead of jumping in, I was stretching a different muscle: I was observing in a new way, a through and above the trees view, not an in the trees view. I could see more things because I wasn't so fixated on fixing things all the time.

And the shipping team didn't just get the orders out, either. They did even better. When faced with the day's mini-emergency (there's always at least one SOS) they served as their own 9-1-1. They realized that some packages needed to be overnighted, and that the UPS guy wasn't arriving to pick them up in time. So they spotted the in-peril parcels, drove them to the UPS store before 6 p.m., and got them en route to their destinations, so they would arrive on time. We're talking about hundreds, if not thousands, of orders that all got shipped out in one fell swoop. Sure, there were some wobbles. There always are. But my perspective had totally changed—I didn't assume any of them were the end of the world.

Plus, as part of my new mission to trust the people in my life, I now had the self-control to not get all up in everyone's business. Even during this shipping dustup, it was clear that they were pretty much crushing it, without me being the bumpers for their bumper cars. And we were going to blow up our target goal. All they really needed was my support and belief in them. Somewhere in there, it dawned on me: *Oh yeah, I guess I could have this sort of a day, any day. I just have to decide not to be as stressed, and to trust people to stay in their lanes and meet the expectations that are now clearly laid out for them. And when someone clearly isn't able to handle their role, either help them to improve, or give them the support to transition into something they'd be happier doing, and find the person who's cherry-picked for the job.*

I called Casey, and it was the opposite from the early months of our relationship, when I'd called him every day—sometimes multiple times a day, huddled on the fire escape outside my first office, teary-voiced and frantic about the latest seemingly fatal fire.

"My team is fucking great!" I said. "My team fucking killed it!"

It was true. And to have had the biggest day in sales unfold, with so many less sandstorms than ever before, was incredible. Nothing amazed me more than when I found myself driving away from the factory at 6:30 p.m. It had only taken seven years, and a million scraped elbows, and bruised egos, but here we were, making it work! It really was an incredible feeling of accomplishment and pride, which I shared with each and every team member. Best of all, I ended the day in my favorite way. As our pig, Oliver, snored nearby (yes, I have a pet potbellied pig, who sleeps on our couch most nights), I shoveled up leftovers with Casey, standing at the island in the kitchen of our home, hashing out everything, making plans for tomorrow, happy as could be.

● ● ●

RATHER THAN MAINTAINING A HAND in every department or possible position, I accepted that we'd taught the team the ropes, so they could be brilliant problem solvers on their own. And I put the focus back where it had started in the first place: on the deeper

6 Ingredients for a True Team

- Clearly designated swim lanes with expectations that are obvious as hell, aka, what do you need and want from that person? CLARITY IS KINDNESS!

- Listening skills on all sides— be able to receive and give feedback.

- Adaptability—being comfortable with the uncomfortable aspects of change, as your team and business grow and shift, because guess what? It happens.

- Humble enthusiasm (it really works in all areas of life).

- Accountability with consequences and positive feedback.

- An overarching goal that everyone is swimming toward.

why of my dream. I doubled down on all the things I was good at—designing a product, telling a story about a product, creating excitement in others—and all the ways I could keep improving, not just as a leader, but as a designer, and as a member of that community of other chefs and dreamers and doers that inspires me every day. There's always more that can be done and learned, always more new things to try and ideas to bring to fruition. We still haven't achieved perfection (if that even exists), but we've definitely made progress! It's all about not trying to control the outcome in order to allow for all of this to happen in its own time.

It doesn't matter how many books you read, or how many hours you spend in coaching, even though that's all great, too. Change can only happen when you DECIDE you are going to upgrade your habits. This can be an uneasy endeavor when you realize that some of the things that got you from Point A to Point B aren't going to get you the rest of the way. For me, it was definitely uncomfortable to acknowledge that all of that hustle, which had gotten me this company and a factory and a staff, wasn't enough. I would still have to keep growing, and learning, and evolving. Um, forever.

Each day, the adventure presents fresh sinkholes. This is not for the faint of heart. But there are ways to get through it, which have made up the Dream First, Details Later perspective that has worked for me.

As long as we're willing to pick ourselves back up and keep at it, we are going to figure out how to make it. You've heard how I did it. Now it's your turn to take your dreaming and start doing.

Ellen's Master To-Do List

☐ **Make a start**, even if it's scary, even if nothing's in place. Figure out the rest from there.

☐ **Put your idea out into the world**, and be willing to learn.

☐ **Do little scary things** to earn notches on your confidence belt.

☐ Show up like a tank, but when the front door isn't open, **climb in through the window**.

☐ **Be your own cheerleader** and share your idea with humble enthusiasm.

☐ **Ask questions, seek feedback, listen hard, and apply** the information you get.

☐ **Own your mistakes**—that's what it means to be a business owner—and keep going.

☐ **Be resourceful** and make use of what you have to get what you don't.

☐ **Expect setbacks** and leap back in anyhow.

☐ **Team up with other dreamers and doers** to get inspired and grow in new ways.

☐ Step out of survival mode—once you've made it, **improve it, again, and again, and again.**

☐ **Find peers who you can be vulnerable with, and don't try to do it all alone.**

☐ **Empower your team members** to shine and then get out of their way to let them do so.

☐ **Try, try again,** in the face of every new challenge, always and forever.

Epilogue

WAKE UP & FIGHT!

➡ **My business was literally born in a restaurant kitchen, and its first goal and deeper purpose was always to serve restaurant cooks—to give them dignity and pride in their role.**

Sure, it has exploded way out beyond the cooking line in the past eight years, but restaurants and their chefs will forever be part of our business, and one close to my heart.

In March 2020, as I began to notice more and more of my favorite restaurants, and apron squad members, close up shop around the world in response to the COVID-19 pandemic, I was paralyzed by fear and uncertainty. We'd already seen a dip in our sales numbers. I knew this situation was not looking good for H&B, too, and I was worried about our team members and how we would take care of them. But amid everything that was happening, and feeling scared for my company, I was also trying to absorb the scale of suffering and loss in the greater world.

On March 17, the stay-at-home order in California went into effect. I slipped into the H&B HQ that day, a Friday, with the idea that I'd be grabbing anything I'd need, for a good long time. No one had any inkling how long that would be. It could be months, maybe longer, before I'd be back at my drawing board. We'd launched a last-minute sale, in the hopes of drumming up whatever business we could, to keep us afloat for as long as it would take. And we knew that we still had to pack up and ship out any and all orders that came in that day by 5 p.m., before we shuttered HQ indefinitely. Casey had come along to be an extra pair of hands, if needed, helping our shipping crew finagle orders and make sure everything got powered down alright.

While I was standing in my office, feeling weird about how quiet the normally cacophonous space was, and overwhelmed by how hard it was to know what I'd need, I stopped and checked my phone. As I

Timeline of a Pivot

FRI, MAR 21, 2020

8:30AM	Head to the office to pack it up for the shutdown
10:00AM	Perusing Instagram and see the Gov Cuomo tweet
NOON	Grab sewer to start playing with sample
1:00PM	Call Dr. Bob, he can't talk.
1:30PM	Make more samples
5:00PM	Call Dr. Bob again. He realized his hospital needs masks too.
6:00PM	Start building out page on website
9:00PM	Finish working sample
9:30PM	Take photos

SAT, MAR 22, 2020

4:00AM	Wake up in a panic. Should we really do this!? Start calling friends to see if we should really do this or not. Gillian gives me a pep talk. Tells me we have to do this.
10AM	Launch mask on the site. Scared shitless.
10:30AM	Sewers come into the factory to reset machines. Alex prints out the patterns.

MON, MAR 24, 2020

ALL DAY	Masks in production: fabric being cut, patterns being printed, markers being made, materials being sourced.

WED, MAR 26, 2020

Start shipping first masks.

• • •

AUGUST 10, 2020 Produced nearly 1 million masks. 275,000 masks donated.

was scrolling through Instagram, a post by the New York City-based fashion designer Christian Siriano caught my eye. NY Governor Andrew Cuomo had announced a critical shortage of face masks and personal protective equipment for health-care and other frontline workers, and the designer had mobilized his sewers to make masks.

I glanced over at our sewing floor, where row after row of sewing machines stood. We had everything we'd need, including racks of cotton and chambray, and a newly nimble product development arm that could pivot with the best of them. Here was something we could DO, not just for H&B as a business, but for doctors and nurses (like my mom), and for regular people, and for the greater good!

I immediately leaped into action, just like I'd done all those years ago when Chef Josef had told me about the woman who was going to make his aprons for him. But now, there was so much more on the line. We were in the midst of an international crisis. Lives were being lost. There was a clear need, and we could fill it—everything else would follow from there. I started Googling masks and making a few quick sketches on the big roll of white paper on my desk. I went to talk to my sewing team about what I was thinking—masks!—as many of them as we could make, and as soon as we could possibly make them—and I asked them to help me figure it out. It was soon clear that we had what it would take to make the masks, but I wanted to be absolutely sure our design was actually worth making. I wanted it to have the same above-and-beyond quality and care as my aprons.

So I called my best friend's husband, Bob Cho, a pediatric surgeon and chief of staff at Shriner's Children's Hospital and asked him what a mask would require to keep people safe.

"We need to do this," I said. "I want to do this. Tell me what you need in a mask. I want to show you what I've got. I'm going to bring it by your house."

He was used to my leaps of urgency by now, but this was a really serious matter.

"I don't know if that's such a good idea," he said. "But I'm super busy right now. I have to take a bunch of calls right now. Let's connect later in the afternoon."

I hung up the phone and got back to work. I was already mid-leap, and there was no grounding me now. By the time Dr. Bob, as I call him, reconnected with me later in the day, I already had six possible patterns to show him. And he had some disturbing news from the front lines: he'd just learned that his entire hospital was running low on supplies, and they needed masks right away now, too.

We both realized: *This actually needed to work.*

It was now Friday afternoon, the same day in which the mask idea had dawned on me. I posted a photo of me in one of our in-progress masks on Instagram, with a note about how we were working on a prototype. It quickly got seven thousand likes and a flurry of positive comments.

Over several FaceTime sessions, Dr. Bob and I worked out the plan for what would become our basic mask, which I named for one of our favorite mottos: Wake Up and Fight. For those people on the front lines, who needed serious protection, the masks could be fit-ted with a filter. No, they would not replace the N95, surgical, or procedural masks mandated by hospitals and health-care facilities. But those masks weren't available in sufficient numbers for everyone who desperately needed them. And our Wake Up and Fight masks could at least be an alternative to offer them. For regular citizens of the world, they would be a great option to wear out in public. With help from the sewing team, by the end of the day, we had our first prototypes. We got in touch with our vendors, to make sure we could really do this. We *could* do this. Were we doing this?! YES, we were already doing it!

By around nine o'clock that night, we'd gone from preparing to close up the factory when we walked in that morning, to preparing to launch a whole new product. After the production team turned

◀

The iPhone photo we posted on our website to pivot the entire company

off the factory lights and rolled down the big garagelike door before the weekend, Casey and I were the last people left in the HQ. We knew we needed to shoot the mask, so we could get it up online. Instead of a typical photo shoot, which takes weeks of planning, emails, and getting several teams involved, we went and grabbed the giant seamless backdrop, which is about eight feet by eight feet, out of our photo studio area. We lugged it through the showroom, around the coffee bar, past the slide, and directly into the kitchen, because that's where there was the best light in the building at night. Casey got down on his hands and knees and used some rolls of toilet paper to fill out the masks, so he could shoot them on his phone. Then, he had me put one on. The photo lights were shining brightly on me. He looked me up and down.

"Maybe smile a little?" he said, in his sweet way.

I just looked at him while raising my eyebrows, but I got his point. I was emotionally exhausted. But I knew he was right. I smiled, but first I ran off, grabbed a tube of mascara, and slashed some on in the dark. As I was jetting from my office back to the kitchen, my eye latched onto a pop of yellow on the product development wall—a bandana I loved. For good measure, I tied it around my neck for some color. Snap. We got our photo.

Forty-five minutes later, we sent it to our senior marketing manager, Aviv, to edit. Using FaceTime we communicated back and forth until we'd gotten all of the details just right. He worked on revamping the photos, taken under pretty subpar conditions, so they looked bright and shiny, like they'd been professionally shot. We drafted some copy with the help of our team and specs from Dr. Bob.

Exhausted, we collapsed into bed at the end of a very long, eventful day. But around four in the morning, I popped up, wide awake. Everything was ready. All we had to do was pull the trigger. I was filled with doubt. *Are we seriously about to do this? Should we be doing this? This is insane.*

But, somewhere deep inside, just like with the aprons, I knew it was right. I knew it was my deeper why as a human. I texted our new, soon-to-be director of ops and asked: "Are you up?" He was in the process of moving from Texas to LA, and I figured he might be. It turned out he wasn't, so I texted my friend Gillian next. As I sat there in the pitch black, worrying about the outcome, and what if it didn't work, she talked me off the ledge. We were taking on a pandemic. This wasn't something simple. This was people's health. But we had to do something. We had to try. I leaped off the dock of my known life and plunged into the unknown, and by Saturday afternoon we'd launched the mask on the H&B website, with a buy-one, donate-one model. For every mask we sold, we would make another one and donate it to a healthcare worker in need.

By the end of the weekend, we'd revamped our sewing floor, not just to make masks instead of aprons, but to social distance every machine, so our sewers were safe while doing their work. We onboarded extra support for customer service, and a third-party warehouse to help us ship masks faster. We tracked down elastic, bought pallets of material, made calls, worked around the clock, with no

◄

Transforming the H&B apron sewing floor into a mask-making operation

reference to what day of the week it was, let alone what time of day. The test kitchen that had once welcomed so many chefs and guests, and which had hosted so many sardine-packed events, was transformed into a secondary shipping station, where masks would be sorted, counted, and prepared for mailing. All done by employees wearing masks, of course—the new normal, at least for this season.

The silver lining is that this pivot allowed us to immediately create and save jobs for our workers, partners, and vendors. One hundred and fifty across LA alone. And then, as we had to reach out to suppliers around the world, who'd shut down their factories, and ask them to reopen to meet our needs, it meant even more jobs. Our supplier in Columbia told us that their factory was employing a thousand people it wouldn't have been able to if it had remained shuttered. In a matter of two months, we'd already produced over half a million masks, and donated two hundred thousand. It felt incredible to be doing something tangible, something helpful to our community, in the face of such overwhelming devastation, and with the knowledge that the restaurant industry may never fully recover to where it once was.

That's the happy, inspiring part of the story.

But the truth is, it's been almost exactly the same journey as the one I took when I started making aprons, all those years ago. Yes, my resources and systems and team are more robust than they've ever been. But I've still taken just as many hockey sticks to the face as I did in the early days of H&B. And there were just as many people yelling at me from the sidelines. While the stakes are even higher. There's no magic formula that's going to make the difficulties go away, even with experience and perspective. But I've got my arsenal of not-so-secret weapons to guide me: the motto of Wake Up and Fight, and the knowledge that a powerful way to make stuff happen is to dream first and figure out the details later. That's exactly what we've done—again.

And yes, plenty has gone wrong. Out of the three hundred thousand masks, sewn, packaged, and shipped to customers around the world, we've had about three thousand complaints. I know that statistically, that's pretty damn good. But it's the unhappy customers who keep me up nights, not just wanting to make them happy, but, always, wanting to be better. Ironically, we're facing a lot of the same problems we had in the early days of our aprons—size issues, fit issues, how to make a mask that can fit everyone like it was designed just for them. Again, the straps have been a headache. Again, we've had to teach people how to wear our masks, how to wash them. We've listened to every single positive comment and complaint we've received about all of these nitty-gritties. We've gone back to the drawing board, and revamped a variety of different aspects, again and again. And we're not done. We'll tweak them, perpetually, until our product is as good as it can be.

Even with all of the skills and experience I've gained, not to mention my incredible support team, it still takes courage to once again leap into the unknown. But I've got a much clearer sense of the bigger why. And while the world is frozen, we are running. Running for ourselves, running for our company, running for our community, and running for each other. And it's scary and it's terrible and it's wonderful. I'm working harder and more than I've ever worked before. And I wouldn't have it any other way.

Just like with our aprons, we've made a lot of mistakes with our masks. But our efforts are coming from an earnest place. And I think that as long as you are earnest about what you're doing, and you explain to people that you're working on it, you're making improvements, they'll meet you halfway.

Some days, I just have to remind myself that we could have said let's just wait this out. But instead we jumped into the ocean and started swimming for our lives, and we are now also helping thousands of people to be safer, to be a part of this Wake Up and Fight movement. It's never just about the product. It's about the why behind whatever it is that you do.

I have so much more context from which to function now, but I'm still not done making mistakes, because living life and going after a goal inevitably comes with bumps, period. The hard truth is that you will never think of every scenario that's going to go wrong. You want to achieve something? Every success has its failures attached to it. You can't do one without the other, and that's OK.

I don't say this to scare you. This is your job as an entrepreneur. This is your job as a human. No matter what happens, you fucking tried. For that you should be proud. Success lies in how bravely you deal with the uncomfortable circumstances as they come up, and how you can be as transparent and helpful and quick to make it right as you possibly can.

The pandemic is a global tragedy. And a micro-tragedy just within the restaurant world itself. Nothing I say here can change that. But what I've come to realize is that there will always be something bigger, a challenge, a need, a call to arms, a reason to wake up and fight. And so, you'd better be ready to go, because the world needs your magic more than you know. See you out there in the sea of life. Let's go go go!

Acknowledgments

➤ **THANK YOU TO:** My deadly effective, powerful, and strong mother, who taught my sister and me to run through the walls of life by never worrying about them and doing it anyway.

My sister Melany, for your giant heart and soulful approach, which has you always flying among the clouds of life. You're a special one.

Mario, my uncle from another mother. I hope you know I'm jamming in as many adventures as I can. Thank you for showing me the way.

Grandpa Hedley & Grandma Elsa, for being so quirky with your tortoises and Great Danes, for drinking tea at 4 p.m., for reading the Encyclopedia Britannica, and Grandma, for always having grace and perfect curls. Wish you were here to see us grow up, but I know you're watching. ♥

My papi, for always reading manuals from front to back, for forcing me to do *Hooked on Phonics*, and for teaching me to drive stick when I was thirteen. You made me earn everything when I was little, and for that, I am eternally grateful.

Casey, my husband and copilot, for being the calm to my storm. When we met, it wasn't like one half meeting another to make a whole. It was two wholes coming together to make five. You're so quite my opposite—we push and we pull, but the result is always forward progress.

Uncle Ted, for the zero judgments to my thousand questions, and for every pep talk, and all of the sandwiches when I really needed them.

Sarah Tomlinson, for spending two years with me, rescheduling every call with a smile, listening to every war story. With your very kind brute force, you dragged me over the finish line. This book was about resilience, and you were a shining example. Truly, thank you for helping me to accomplish a bucket list item in writing a book, and turning a spaghetti ball of thoughts into something that will hopefully inspire others. I legitimately could not have done it without you.

ACKNOWLEDGMENTS

Nicole Tourtelot, for being so much more than an agent; you're more like a life coach. In so many ways, you were the air traffic controller for what this book could become. Typically, I convince others, but you convinced me; I really admire that, and I learned so much from you. Thank you.

Leah Trouwborst, for fighting for this book, and always approaching whatever we threw at you with curiosity and a desire to make it better. You led us, but you also got right in the trenches with us, helping us to work things through and figure them out, and make a book that will hopefully inspire people to get more out of life.

The whole Portfolio team, especially Niki Papadopoulos. And especially, *especially* Adrian Zackheim; from our first meeting, you stole the room with your energy and perspective; I knew you were my kind of guy. It meant so much that you fully understood where I was coming from. I couldn't have been prouder or happier to join the Portfolio family. For me, Portfolio is the epitome of serious, well-done publishing, and Adrian, you're such a big part of that, and do things so well.

Alaina Sullivan, for helping us to bring the book to life with your visual storytelling, taking what I saw in my head and putting it on paper, in a way that even I couldn't explain. You plugged in perfectly, as if you had been there all along, and completed the book with your visuals.

My H&B team for being such professionals while relentlessly pursuing our next chapter. You inspire me every day. The O.G. H&B squad, especially Kevin, Daisha, Allie, Marissa, Rachel, Noelle, Marty, John. Thank you for sharing a chapter of your life with a chapter of mine. #ForeverApronSquad #ForeverHustle

All who believed in H&B and helped along the way, especially: Iain Shovlin, Nona Farahnik Yadegar, John Adler, Aleksey Berezin, Patty Rodriguez, Richard & Jazmin Blais, Gavin Kaysen, Caue Suplicy (Barnana), Ben Goldrisch, Evan Funke, Aaron Silverman, Omid Davoodi, Gary Fleck, Marc Vetri, Dana Cowin & Barclay, Courtney Smith, Denise Restari, Shelley Phillips, Nic Tran, Chris Toy, Billy Dureny, Darren Litt, Chuck Berk, Ricky Schlesinger, Stephanie Izzard, Iris Caplowe, Brett Shirreffs, Ali Cayne, Josef Centeno, Alton Brown, Bryan Voltaggio, Michael Voltaggio, Nancy Silverton, Neil Fraser, David Chang, Martha Stewart, Jonathan Waxman, Neil and Cath, Garret, Diane, Tori, Ryan, Becca, Jasmine, Brittany.

▲ **In my kitchen at home, smiling ear to ear for *The New York Times***

About the Author

━━➤ Ellen Marie Bennet is the founder and CEO of @hedleyandbennett, an apron and kitchen gear brand that makes proper, badass aprons and gear for people who love to cook. She was a line cook at Bäco Mercat and two-Michelin-starred Providence in Los Angeles when she got inspired to upgrade their aprons. H&B's iconic ampersand is now worn in restaurant kitchens and by home cooks everywhere. Collaborations have sprung up with Rifle Paper Co., Vans, Madewell, and more. Ellen's adventures can be followed on Instagram @ellenmariebennett. She lives in Los Angeles with her husband, Casey, their pig, Oliver (@oliverspigadventures), and their five chickens.